CHAPTER 1

The Carefree Days

B & B

"**P**ut the cloth on, Penny; your father's coming."

Penny hastily set the table, reflecting as she did so on what a strange match her parents were. Her bearded father, so strict and forbidding; her mother, so neat, petite, and soft-spoken. She had heard the tale in the village of how her mother had threatened to return home to her folks if this strange man who had courted her for so long did not make up his mind and marry her.

"She must have had the spirit to stand up to him, then," Penny reflected.

But once married, he had soon become a dominant force in his household. Subjected to his tantrums, she gradually sank into subjection, until by now, his every whim was granted. She had long since learnt to make a show of having the meal ready, by laying the table and prodding the potatoes. If it was not ready, his temper, aided by the beer he had consumed before returning home, would thunder through the little cottage.

Bill Thompson was a regular at the White Goose and a crack shot on their shooting team; he was also held in high esteem in the local Methodist chapel. Sunday would see him leaving the pub and wending his way homeward to his terraced cottage, where Lizzie, his wife, would have a large roast ready for him. Penny, their eldest, would help her mother dish up the meal, while Martha, two years younger, kept baby Jane quiet. Their father's bright blue eyes beneath those shaggy eyebrows twinkled merrily when he was amused. But if the children were to speak without being spoken to, they flashed with anger cold as steel.

After dinner had been eaten, he would have a sleep. Penny and her sisters stayed very quiet on this, the Sabbath day. There was no playing, for their clothes must be kept clean for chapel.

The Good Book and the *Christian Herald* was available, if they felt inclined to read. Penny was soon lost in daydreams, which she would wake from with a start, to hear her mother calling, "Give me a hand with the tea, girls, and don't forget to wash your hands."

By four o'clock, they had had tea, for at 5:30 precisely, the family would file down through the village to chapel, Father in his hard hat, which he doffed to passers-by, with Mother on his arm and the two girls behind, wheeling the baby in her carriage.

In summer, when it was dry, they would go for a walk after chapel, but never very far, as there was always someone Father would stop to talk to. When at last the handshaking and blessings were over, time was always a little short. For Bill Thompson, despite his faults, was a hard-working man who arose early to tend his crops. So it was early to bed for all the family.

The smallholding was a short distance from the cottage. He took most of the produce to market in nearby Hastings. The horse and cart had to be made ready and the crops freshly gathered. Then there was a long haul up White Hart Hill, where the horse would need to rest halfway. The life was hard, with small returns for his labours, and yet he was happy, having been born to raise a living from the soil.

At the end of the garden was the pigsty where the pig lived. And when it was slaughtered, Penny and Martha would help their mother to salt the meat, make brawn from the head, scald the intestines, and make them into sausages with the oddments. That week, there would be fresh liver, chitterlings, fries, trotters, sausages, and brawn. For later, salt pork and a side of bacon; nothing was wasted.

On the smallholding, their father also raised hens and a few ducks. These would be eaten when the new potatoes and green peas were ready. At the end of the laying season, there would be the odd boiling fowl. Always when the flush of eggs came in March, some would be laid down in a

The House on the Green

Betty S. Hilton

author**HOUSE**

AuthorHouse™ UK
1663 Liberty Drive
Bloomington, IN 47403 USA
www.authorhouse.co.uk
Phone: UK TFN: 0800 0148641 (Toll Free inside the UK)
        UK Local: 02036 956322 (+44 20 3695 6322 from outside the UK)

Published by AuthorHouse 11/19/2020

ISBN: 978-1-6655-8253-7 (sc)
ISBN: 978-1-6655-8254-4 (hc)
ISBN: 978-1-6655-8252-0 (e)

Library of Congress Control Number: 2020923344

Print information available on the last page.

This book is printed on acid-free paper.

CONTENTS

water glass for use in winter, when eggs would be in short supply. Being a good shot, they were never short of pigeons and pheasants, and they snared rabbits too. They ate good, wholesome food.

Penny and Martha often went to the windmill on Hog Hill in Panel Lane to fetch flour. They played there among the bags of grain with the miller's two sons. Then homeward they would hurry to Mother, who had the oven warm and the yeast ready for baking. They loved to help her with this. The smell of the fresh loaves and tea cakes hung in the air. When all was finished, Mother would take two hot rolls, split them, and place a knob of homemade butter on each, giving them to Penny and Martha as their reward.

During the week in term time, Penny and Martha were to be found learning the three Rs at the village school. Mr Day, the long-suffering schoolmaster, taught a class whose ages ranged from five years old to fourteen.

As Penny's fourteenth birthday approached, she was forced to seek employment; she had always been a hare-brained child, with never a thought for the future. Work was scarce. Her mother, who had been in service as a maid, decided to give her daughter a better chance in life by sending her to be an assistant to a dressmaker in Winchelsea. Poor Penny, she who had loved to run through the fields and woods, now had a three-mile walk to a cramped workroom. Here she had to fit the paper patterns, do the hemming up, and make alterations to sweat-stained clothes. She hated every moment of it. It soon became apparent that she had no aptitude for this trade, and the dressmaker asked her mother to take her back.

After a short spell at home, Penny became a shop assistant. In the usual attire of a black dress, white collar, and cuffs, she was now employed by a large family of drapers in the nearby town of Hastings. For the first time, she was unable to travel home and stayed in a cheap boarding house all week; the food was poor compared with what she had been used to. But on Saturday evening after the shop closed, she would hurry to George Street, where the local carrier was waiting to leave for White Hart Hill with his collections of parcels. Sitting beside Len she'd clutch her small bag and watch the steam rising from the nostrils of the fine pair of horses, resplendent in their brasses, as they struggled up the steep hill to Ore and then on until they came to the sharp bends of Bachelors Bump, then onward to White Hart Hill.

Here, the carrier would apply the brakes. And on dark nights, she could see the sparks fly from the brake shoes, like fireflies. The smell of the sweat rising from the horses' backs mingled with the smell of the fields. They travelled through the village of Guestling and on to the Thorn, then home.

Penny was now a young woman of nearly seventeen; like most young ladies, she put her hair up and dressed in a fine calico and lace ruffle blouse, with a long black taffeta skirt; she was a decided hit with the local young men. An attractive girl of high spirits, and many were the farmer's sons swayed by her charms. Penny wished to see so much more of life. She and Eve applied to be maids in London. Before they set off for their respective posts, Penny's mother, who knew the pitfalls of being in service, told her what to expect:

"Beware of taking wine with the menservants or the sons of the house, lest you lose your honour. Never go out with a young man unless you have been properly introduced, and beware of getting into conversations with strangers on the journey or in the London station."

At last, the day for their departure dawned; she kissed her family and waved goodbye to them and her beloved Sussex, with its gentle rolling fields and woods, where she had run and played as a child. Seated beside the carrier, who was to take them to the station, both girls were quiet with their thoughts. Clutching their cloth bags with their few possessions, they were both apprehensive and excited. This then was the start of a great adventure beyond the horizon they had always known.

CHAPTER 2

A New Horizon

~ & ~

Penny remembered her mother's warning and was more than a little alarmed when her young friend was drawn into conversation with two young men on the train. Penny, for all her localised education, was a good judge of character, and there was just something about them she did not trust. When they disembarked at Victoria Station, the young men suggested they all have a drink together. Penny declined, saying she still had a long way to go to her position in Hammersmith. Her friend tried to persuade her, but she was adamant in her refusal. Her friend refused to accompany Penny, turning to go with the young men. Reluctantly, Penny went on her way, for she had yet to find her destination and knew she must arrive before dark.

Lugging her cloth bag, Penny walked the streets of Hammersmith, looking for the house. At last, she came to a tall sombre building that cast a melancholy shadow on the street. Plucking up courage, she mounted the steps and pulled the large brass bell; after what seemed an eternity, the door opened. A tall, angular woman, with an expressionless face, ushered her in.

"You're the new maid, I suppose?"

"Yes," Penny replied.

Without another word, the woman strode off and began walking up the stairs. Penny followed until they reached the fourth and last floor. The woman threw open a door to a small, white-washed room. Inside was an iron bedstead, a chair, and a two-drawer chest on which sat a jug and bowl; a chamber pot rested on the floor. That was it; bare boards, no curtains to keep out the draughts, a bleak start indeed.

"When you have unpacked, you can help Cook with dinner. You will wash up before you learn to turn down the master's bed."

Having given her orders, Miss Stonehouse, for this was the haughty woman's name, turned on her heel and stomped downstairs, keys chinking on the chatelaine she wore at her waist.

Left on her own at last, Penny felt the big adventure had gone very flat. She was tired and hungry. Above all, she wished she had not left her friend. They had promised their mothers to stay together. But there was no going back now. What was done could not be undone.

Penny settled into her job, and if she did not like it, at least it was a job at a time when many had no employment at all. Her day started at 5:30 a.m., when she had breakfast in the servant's room below stairs, in the company of the kitchen maid, serving maid, and odd job man. This was presided over by Miss Stonehouse, who would discuss the day's duties with the odd job man while the three girls chatted to each other.

Penny's mother had been right to fear for the girls, as it now appeared that her friend was missing. She was never heard of again. Penny feared she may have been taken by white slavers, who found country girls easy prey. It was a terrible shock to Penny, and she became very cautious when making friends.

Penny got on well with the other two girls; when their duties for the day were over, the three of them would sit in the servant's room, chatting and sewing. On Saturdays, Penny finished early, and sometimes, she and one of the other maids (for one always had to remain to serve supper) would go to the music hall or on a tram ride; in the summer, they'd go down by the river to watch the boats.

Sunday afternoon, they had off; if the weather was fine, they would make for one of the parks and watch the fashions of the rich ladies out for a stroll. They would copy some of the ideas, trimming a hat or adding lace or a tuck to their own Sunday best. A trip to the park was wonderful relaxation after dragging up and down stairs all week.

At first, Penny tried going to chapel, as had been her habit for so many years, but the stone-pillared building was so cold and unwelcoming after the little chapel at home.

She was homesick, especially when the spring daffodils were out in the parks. She would think of the primroses covering the banks along the Sussex Lanes. But there was no turning back. There was no work at home, and her mother was hard put to it to make ends meet.

After Penny had been in London for a year, she could go home for one week. She had been saving for her fare since her arrival and was able to buy her parents and sisters each a small present: Father a new pipe, Mother a tiny bottle of perfume, and a lace-edged handkerchief for each of her sisters.

When the day of her departure arrived, it was pouring with rain, but nothing could dampen her spirits. She was going home. Riding to the station in the tram, she felt suddenly free. With a little money in her pocket, she was escaping back to the rolling green fields, where she had been so happy.

London had been a great disappointment to Penny. You needed wealth and position to enjoy the city life. There was little to enjoy in the sombre house in Hammersmith.

"I will not go back to climbing those dreadful stairs and working so hard," she told her mother.

Her mother shook her head sadly and said, "If only you had worked harder at the dressmakers, you could have taken in work on your own account now."

The week passed quickly, and Penny, whose money had run out by now, was forced to return to her job. She began avidly searching the situations vacant columns in the newspapers. At last she saw, "Wanted, Smart young woman to housekeep for elderly invalid wife and her doctor husband."

Feeling desperate, she put on her coat and hat, grabbed her purse, and ran from the house. Echoing behind her, she heard the housekeeper's harsh voice utter, "Where do you think you're going?"

But she did not look back; it was a now or never.

Spending her last few pennies on the tram fare, Penny made her way to the doctor's house in Chelsea. A fine Georgian residence, it stood back from the road. A semi-circular gravel drive with double gates enabled a carriage to be quickly at the door and away without the bother of backing horses. That day, as Penny arrived, the carriage was at the door, and the doctor, carrying his black bag, nearly collided with Penny on the steps. "Good gracious, girl," he said. "Can't you see I'm in a hurry? Out of the way."

Penny turned in time to catch sight of the young driver smiling down at her, giving her a thumbs-up. He had a round, jolly face and very blue eyes, and with a swish of the reins, they were away at great speed.

"Who were you wanting to see, miss?" asked the maid who had come to shut the gates.

"I came about the job," Penny replied.

"There is only the mistress, and she is in bed today. Will you wait until the doctor returns or come back tomorrow?"

"May I wait?" Penny knew she couldn't come again tomorrow. Heaven knows how she was going to get back to Hammersmith tonight anyway, with all her money gone.

She sat in the great hallway, waiting, taking in her surroundings; it was a light, airy hall with a high ceiling of patterned plaster. The wide staircase swept gently upwards to the landing, where Corinthian pillars stretched up to the ceiling. The plaster was patterned, Penny thought, like an iced wedding cake. The thick pile of the carpet made moving about quite quiet.

After a while, Penny arose and walked carefully around the hall, looking at the pictures and the fine pieces of porcelain in the rosewood cabinet. Just then, the door burst open, and there stood the doctor. "You are still here then?" he asked.

Penny turned and said, "Good evening, sir. I came in answer to your advertisement for a housekeeper."

"Did you, now? Well, don't you think you are rather young for such responsibility?"

"Oh no," Penny said. "I am a very efficient housekeeper."

The doctor smiled and said, "You look very, young to me, but I like your spirit. You can come on a month trial, then. When can you start?"

"May I start straight away, please?" Penny asked.

The doctor looked surprised.

"You see, sir, I spent the last of my money to get here. I am afraid to return to Hammersmith. I dashed here as soon as I saw the paper. The housekeeper is a real dragon; she will have my skin if I return so late."

He laughed and said, "As I thought, you are only a maid. However, you shall stay. Molly will take care of you tonight, and tomorrow, we can take you to collect your things."

He rang the bell, and the maid Penny had seen earlier appeared.

"Molly give this young lady something hot to eat," he said. "Then see to it that she has a bed and some clean linen." He turned to Penny and said, "Good evening, young lady. I will see you in the morning when we can sort out details."

"Thank you, sir," she replied.

"Come with me, please, miss," Molly said.

Penny followed her through to the kitchen, where simmering gently on the range was a large stock pot full of stew. Penny sat at the large deal table, where Molly served her a plate of piping hot stew. She then set a tray with a serving for the doctor. "He likes something warming when he comes in," she told Penny. "Will should be in for some too, soon as he has bedded the horses down."

So, the round-faced young man who had smiled at Penny was Will. Penny, remembering him, smiled to herself. This was certainly a friendly household, she thought.

After a while, he came in. She was struck by how tired he looked, but the blue eyes still twinkled at her.

"Hello," he said. "Have you come to join us, then?"

"I hope so," Penny replied. "I am on a month trial as housekeeper."

"It will be a trial too; have you met Her Majesty yet?"

"No, is she very difficult, then?"

Molly burst out laughing and replied, "Is she difficult? You must be joking."

Will looked thoughtful. "One thing I will say, though; the doctor's alright, but life can't be easy for him. She suffers a lot of pain too."

Will relapsed into silence. Penny now realised this was the reason she had been given a chance. Maybe the doctor had trouble keeping a housekeeper if his wife was demanding. If only she could hold on to this job, she would be able to keep house in future instead of being at everyone's beck and call as a maid. This was her lucky break, and she meant it to stay that way.

Supper finished, Penny said goodnight to Will, and Molly took her through the kitchen and up the back stairs to her room. Decorated in a floral paper with chintz curtains at the window and a carpeted floor, it was a cheerful and warm change from her room in the house at Hammersmith. Furnished with a bed covered with a paisley coverlet, and containing a chest of drawers, cupboard with hanging space for clothes, and a washstand, complete with basin and jug, there was also a very cosy button-back chair.

"Goodnight, miss," Molly said, smiling. "I will call you in the morning."

"Thank you, Molly, that would be kind of you."

She felt among friends. She had been good friends with the other girls at Hammersmith, but the regime of Miss Stonehouse was a hard one, and living conditions very spartan.

Crossing to the window, Penny opened it and looked out. In the moonlight, she could see the shapes of the trees and a path edged by flower borders. She caught the fragrant smell of honeysuckle, reminding her of home, where it grew wild in the woods and hedgerows. Snuffing out the lamp, she lay down and was soon in a dreamless sleep.

CHAPTER 3

The Doctor's House

B ❦ B

S he woke suddenly. Whatever was that noise in the middle of the night? There it was again. Thump! Thump! And someone shouting. She struggled out of bed and lit the lamp. Covering herself with her coat, she descended the stairs. Will sat in the kitchen, pulling on his boots.

"Mrs Jackson's baby is on the way," he said. "Have the kettle on for when we get back; master will need a hot drink."

With that, he was gone; Penny could hear the horse and carriage being drawn up outside. Then the door banged, and with a loud "Gee up!" they were gone.

She returned to the kitchen and lit the lamps; after filling the kettle, she opened the dampers on the range and made up the fire.

Taking up her lamp, she decided to go up to her room and dress. As she reached the landing outside her door, a strange man rushed past, bumping into her. In her effort to stop the lamp flaring, she missed the features of the man, but as she turned, she saw his back as he slipped out of the back door into the garden.

She quickly made her way along the passage to what she presumed was Molly's room. Opening the door, she saw that this was a man's room, probably Will's. At the end of the passage was another door. She knocked gently and went in. Molly was in bed, apparently asleep, but she wasn't fooled. With all the commotion of the last hour, sleep would have been quite impossible.

She shook the girl by the shoulder and called, "Wake up."

Yawning, Molly sat up and asked, "What's the matter?"

"Mrs Jackson's baby is on the way. I have made up the fire, put on the kettle, and lit the lamps. When I came upstairs to dress, someone, a man, nearly knocked me over on the landing. Do you think it was a burglar? Should I get the police?"

"Oh, no, miss," Molly cried. "Please don't do that. It was Joe, my boyfriend. That's why I didn't come down. I thought if I pretend not to wake up, Joe could slip out as soon as a carriage left."

Penny could see the other girl's face was very red. "Oh, you silly girl; do you hope to marry him?"

"I can't; he's married already, but his wife doesn't understand him."

"I expect she does, only too well," was Penny's only comment.

"Well, don't tell," the girl asked, looking imploringly at Penny.

Back in her room, Penny dressed thoughtfully. She certainly didn't want to get involved with any man. All she wanted was a chance to do well for herself and prove to her parents that she wasn't as hare-brained as they supposed.

She dressed, went downstairs, and busied herself in the kitchen. After a while, she heard, the sound of carriage wheels on the gravel, and then the doctor came in. He looked pale and drawn; he lowered himself into a chair and pulled off his boots.

"It's been a hard night," he said, and taking his cup of steaming cocoa, he went out.

Penny made another cup ready for Will. He came in, looking sad.

"How did it go?" she asked.

"Lost them both," he replied softly. "It was her twelfth child. Place was terrible, husband drunk, all the kids in two rooms, and no hot water. Good grief, it makes you sick to see how some of them live. Poor little bastards. It will be the union for them now."

He seemed hurt but also angry. Penny wondered what kind of background he came from; his manner of speaking was rough, but it was obvious he had a good heart.

Will drank up and said, "Ah well, better get another couple of hours' kip." He smiled at Penny and added, "You should too; you need to snatch it when you can in this job. Molly usually does these days. It was a treat to come home to something hot tonight."

Penny felt a stab of annoyance with Molly. No doubt she had feigned sleep on other occasions too.

Morning soon came, and Penny awoke to see Molly drawing back the curtains. The sun streamed in.

"Seven o'clock, miss. We have breakfast now with Will. Doctor has his sent up too, but the mistress won't have hers until nine."

Polly sat up, still weary after last night's excitement. "Right, Molly. I'll be down straight away."

Nothing was mentioned of the night before. They sat around the table, eating in comparative silence. Will looked thoughtful and Molly seemed sullen this morning. Penny was glad of the silence. She would be happy to be over the ordeal of fetching her things.

"Are you fit?" Will asked, looked across at Penny. "Better fetch those things of yours before he finishes his surgery."

Suddenly, she realised, Will must be back in time for the doctor's rounds. So, leaving Molly to do the dishes, she hurried upstairs for her coat.

It did not take them long to arrive at the Hammersmith house, as being early, they missed most of the traffic. "Shall I come with you?" Will offered, smiling. "Wouldn't like the Dragon to get you."

Penny laughed and said, "I wish you would. It might help me get out quicker."

Miss Stonehouse came to the door. "Well, I might have known," she snapped. "Disgraceful, running off like that. A decent girl would wait until she was married. Collect your things and get out."

Penny hurried up those stairs for the last time, hardly able to keep from laughing. One look at Will's bewildered face had been enough. Obviously, Miss Stonehouse thought she had spent the night with him.

As they drew away from the house, she was able to wave goodbye to the two other maids, who were peeping from the kitchen windows. She had not had a chance to speak to them. She was determined to seek them out in the park on Sunday.

Back at the house, surgery was finished, and the doctor called Penny into his study.

"How did you get on, then, young lady?" he asked.

Penny told him of the encounter with the housekeeper, and of Will's embarrassment. He roared with laughter.

"No good applying for a reference in that quarter," he said. "I shall have to trust you." Then he explained what duties he expected her to perform, and what time off she could have, and what wages to expect.

Penny felt at ease with the doctor, as he had such a kindly disposition.

"Now I want you to meet my wife; she is looking forward to seeing you."

He led her up the stairs into a large, brightly lit room. A frail figure sat in a wheelchair by the window overlooking the garden.

"This is our new housekeeper, dear."

Penny felt herself being scrutinised by a pair of very blue eyes with the same steely glint that her father's,held, a slight woman, aged beyond her years by her disabilities. Her white hair framed a face racked with pain. Penny at once felt compassion for her.

"Good morning, ma'am," she said. "I am pleased to meet you. I will do my best to serve you, ma'am."

"How old are you, child?"

"Nearly twenty," Penny replied.

"Ah, so young; youth, it is so fleeting. But you look strong, which is something I never was. A doctor's household is always at beck and call. Do you really think you can cope?"

"Yes, I'm sure I can," she replied.

"Good, then I will leave you to organise everything. Molly is a good girl to work with, but you must keep an eye on her, or you'll find yourself taking the greatest burden."

"Thank you," Penny said. "I'll remember that." She thought of last night. Yes, Molly would need to be pushed, but gently.

"Come and see me when you get spare time," she said. "I like to keep in touch with events."

Promising to do this, Penny took her leave and returned to the kitchen. Her determination had not been dampened by her interview with the doctor's wife. She immediately set about organising the household and spent the next several weeks keeping things running smoothly.

After a month, the doctor called her into his study and said, "Come in and sit down, Penny. I wanted to have a word with you; my wife and I are very pleased with your efforts to run this difficult household, so in token of appreciation, we are raising your salary a little."

"Thank you, sir." Penny was thrilled; she had managed to get through her trial period, and the extra money meant she could put a little away. That night, she wrote off to her mother and father to let them know her good fortune.

On many evenings, Will would come and sit in the kitchen and chat with her. And then, it became a regular thing for them to spend Wednesday afternoons together (this was the doctor's half-day). Will was always great fun to be with, always ready with a joke and a kind word when things were not going so well. She had taken to mending his clothes after seeing him twist his socks around so that his heel was covered. He was ambitious and often talked of making his fortune. On one occasion, he told her his elder brother had sailed for Canada, adding that he was seriously thinking of doing the same.

Penny looked so upset at this suggestion that he asked, "Would you miss me so much, then? You looked right sad."

But with a toss of her head, she snapped, "I'll not fret over any man."

But he never spoke of it again.

Three months passed since Penny began working for the doctor; one night, going up to bed, she heard muffled sobs coming from Molly's room. She tapped gently on the door and then went in. Molly was sitting on the bed, crying as if her heart would break.

"What is it, Molly? Can I help?"

"Oh, miss, I am in trouble."

The poor girl looked at Penny with eyes that were red with weeping.

"What shall I do? Joe wants nothing more to do with me now. He does not want his wife to hear of me. I've been a fool; I thought he loved me."

Tears streamed down her face. Penny had thought this affair would have a sad ending, but seeing Molly's distress and knowing how she had loved Joe, she felt only pity for her.

"Have you any family who you could turn to?" she asked.

"No. My mother is dead, and Father has remarried."

"Then we must tell the doctor," Penny concluded, "and see what he suggests."

When the girls approached their employer, he was sympathetic.

"Tell Molly she can stay until the baby is due," he said. "Then I can get her into hospital. But I can't let her return to this house with the baby. It would be too inconvenient to have a baby here with emergencies at night and an invalid wife."

So Molly stayed, and she and Penny knitted and sewed for the baby during the evenings while Will sat reading and smoking his pipe. On occasion, he found himself watching Penny sewing the small garments and thinking what a good wife she would make. But he always dismissed these thoughts. He was certain she would never consider a rough fellow like himself.

Penny, for her part, had grown very fond of Will. She no longer noticed his rough, manner; she only saw his kindness.

As the time for the baby drew near, Molly grew worried, for she had nowhere to go when she left hospital. Unless she could find a job, both she and the baby would have to go into the union.

One night, Penny was seated at the table, engrossed in the household accounts, when she heard Molly exclaim, "Oh, my back."

Molly had been making the fire up, but now she had both hands pressed to her back; she cried, "It has started, I think."

Will put on his boots to fetch the horse and carriage. Penny called the doctor and then went upstairs to retrieve Molly's case, containing her possessions and the baby's clothes they had made. "Good luck, Molly," she said when she came back down. "I will come and see you. God Bless."

She did not know what else to say. Molly nodded, eyes swimming with tears. Watching the carriage leave brought a lump to Penny's throat. If only there was some way to help her.

When the doctor returned, he was smiling; he said, "It was an eight-pound boy, Penny. You would be pleased to know there was a lady at the hospital who was unable to feed her baby; she offered Molly a position as a wet nurse. She will be paid quite a good sum, and her baby will be fostered out; it should give her a chance to get on her feet."

"But what of Molly's baby, Doctor? He needs his mother's milk."

"He is a strong child," he replied. "With care, he can be reared. I can see no other solution except the workhouse for them both, and he would be unlikely to survive there."

The following Wednesday, the doctor lent Will the carriage for the afternoon.

"Where shall we go, Penny?" Will asked.

"Well, we could call and see Molly, and then go for a ride."

Will sighed and said, "Alright, but don't stay too long. I like you to myself sometimes, you know."

The place where Molly was working was very grand; a uniformed maid answered the door. They were shown up to the nursery. Molly looking very pale and wane, but was very pleased to see them.

"How is little Joe?" Penny asked.

"I don't know. The mistress has him out to be fostered. She says it would be better if I don't see him for a while. But oh, how I worry if he is alright."

"We could pop round and see him, couldn't we, Will?"

Before Will could answer, Molly said, "Would you? It would be such a weight off my mind." She smiled with relief.

"Come on, then, Penny; let's get on, or I'll have no time on my own with you."

Molly laughed. "Do you need a chaperone, Penny?"

The afternoon drifted by, and Will was feeling exasperated. He had been waiting for this opportunity; now, it was going to be wasted. He had made up his mind to ask Penny to marry him. Instead, he was spending his time baby visiting. He began to whistle between his teeth.

Presently, he felt her hand on his as he held the rein. "Gently, Will," Penny said kindly. "I know how you feel, but we must think of Molly."

"Blow Molly," Will exploded. "All I think about is you, Penny. I wanted to take you somewhere nice and asked you to marry me."

"I thought you'd never ask," Penny said, giggling; once she started, there was no stopping her.

"I mean it," he shouted, so loudly that the horse took off at a gallop, tipping Penny over backwards. He started to laugh; what a funny sight she looked, feet in the air, petticoats showing.

They soon came to the address where little Joe was fostered. It was a tenement building in a festering slum. Children hung about outside, looking pale and hungry. Tired-looking women shuffled by, carrying firewood and pieces of vegetables dropped by the porters in the fruit and vegetable market.

Across the way, singing came from the pub, followed by the crash of breaking glass, as a fight broke out.

"Blimey," said Will. "What a dump."

"Come on," Penny said. "We must go and see little Joe now we are here."

They found the address on the top floor. As they climbed the stairs, she found herself thinking of the fresh air and green fields of home. These children did not stand a chance. No wonder so many died of consumption, living in these squalid conditions. She loved Will, but she would not marry him until they could have a decent home. No way would she bring children into the world to live like this.

The woman who answered the door smiled when they said they had come to see little Joe.

"Come in," she said. "You'll be wanting a cuppa after your journey."

The room was clean, but untidy; the woman was very pleasant and seemed happy to see them. Little Joe was asleep in the drawer of a chest. He looked pale but cared for.

"I do hope your friend won't take him back," the woman said. "We lost our own boy with the fever. We've really grown to love him."

Penny felt uncomfortable. Sorry for the woman. But sorrier for Joe, who must now be strong enough to survive in this slum, where infection lurked at every turn.

Back at the doctor's that night, Will smoked his pipe and sat thoughtfully. "Have you thought anymore about marrying me, then?" he asked.

"Yes, I have," Penny replied. "And the answer is no. Not because I do not love you, but because we have no money and nowhere to go. I do not want to end up raising kids in a slum. I want my children to grow up without rickets and with fresh air in their lungs. I never really thought about it when I was home. My mum and dad fed us well. We always had a good fire, and decent clothes. It must have been hard for them to provide what they did, and we had the fields to play in. I had a good childhood. I must do the same for my children."

"You were lucky," Will replied. "There were seven of us, so there wasn't so much to go around. My dad liked his booze too. But I guess we did not do too badly. It is city kids that have it rough. But we don't have to stay in London."

Nothing more was said, it was as if there was an unspoken promise between them. Will knew she loved him, and he was going to find a way to make his dreams come true.

CHAPTER 4

Tom Returns from the Wild

B & B

One morning, there was a letter for Will. He sat and read it over breakfast. "What do you think?" he said to Penny. "My brother has written. He is on his way home from Canada."

"Has he been gone long?" Penny asked.

"Close on two years. Mum will be pleased to see him. She has worried herself sick, not knowing where he was or if he was safe."

It was nearly three months before Tom arrived to see Will, who was shocked to see how strained and tired his brother looked.

When he expressed his concern, Tom replied, "You'd be tired too, if you had been through what I've been through."

Tom told of how he had set off to be a trapper in a part of Canada inhabited only by Indians. The winter was long and cold, and the summer was hot, and mosquito infested. He encountered bears and a savage wolverine that tore down the shed door, trying to eat his dogs. "He would have eaten me, too, if I hadn't shot him first."

Tom stayed and visited until it was quite late. Penny and Will really enjoyed his company and hearing about his exciting adventures. Will felt a little envious. A glimmer of an idea was taking shape in his mind. Perhaps he should push the boat out and take a chance on life; he had not seen any of the world yet. He might find a way to make his fortune. Tom had not done that, but he had had some great experiences, and he looked smart, so he must have earned a bit. On his next day off, he went on his own to see Tom.

After opening his door, Tom ushered Will into a room where several other young men were sitting in a circle, talking earnestly. "This is my brother Will," he said.

"Pleased to meet you, Will," someone said. "Are you going to join us on this expedition, then?"

"I haven't heard about it," he replied. "Where are you going, then?"

The young man laughed and said, "Tell him, Tom." Tom smiled let me introduce Will to you all,,Phillip, Callum, Mike, this is my brother.

"We're going to Dawson City," Tom added "to fetch a load of gold dust."

They talked until late in the night. Two of them had already been to Canada. One of them, Philip, was convinced that with the right gear and provisions, they would find their fortunes.

"Count me in," Will said. "I'm willing to give it a go."

"It will need a lot of preparation," Philip said, "and we shall need a good outfit each and quite a bit of cash for emergencies. That was our trouble before. The supplies you buy there are sold at inflated prices. We could take our own oxen out. Then we could eat them or sell them when they have carried our stuff over the trail."

This young man didn't look in the least bit able to handle a donkey, let alone oxen. But he was fired with enthusiasm.

"Why not buy them in Seattle and ship them up to Anchorage from there?" suggested Tom. "First, we must get some money together."

Will was very, excited; it would be a wonderful adventure. Now he had to convince Penny.

When Penny heard the proposal, she thought them completely mad.

"You don't even know how to manage oxen. And another thing: It's one of the coldest places on earth; it will be a terrible journey."

But she could not dissuade Will, who said, "I know it's risky. But I'll never get another chance like this. I want to go. I promise if I haven't made it in two years, I'll come home. Will you wait for me?"

"Well, I don't have much say in the matter, do I?"

During the next three months, Tom did everything he could to save money. Gradually, the group got together their outfits and sixty pounds each in cash.

Penny didn't think this was enough; after reconciling with the fact that he was going, she said, "I have eighty pounds saved, and I want you to take it with you. It is my insurance that you have enough if it doesn't work out."

"Alright, but it is only a loan, mind. Thank you, love."

Will was looking forward to the trip but had been unsure about Penny. But now, he was sure she would be true to him.

At last, the day of departure arrived. The doctor allowed Penny the day off to see the brothers and their friends depart. When she saw Will turn and wave from the top of the gangplank, she had a lump in her throat and tear-filled eyes. Would they ever be together again, she wondered; had she been foolish not to marry him when he had asked? Was she asking for too much? Now he was facing danger in the hope of making his fortune. And he may never come back. Amidst the hooting of the ship's siren, the ropes cast off, and the ship weighed anchor.

Will and his companions disappeared into the crowd. They were travelling steerage to save money. Now Will was gone, Penny felt very low on the train returning to London; emptiness consumed her every thought.

Why did he have to go? she asked herself, but she knew he had to get the urge to travel out of his system before he could settle down. He was trying hard not to fall into the poverty trap that kept so many imprisoned for life. He may never find his fortune, but his experiences would remain with him, and he would be able to say, "I tried."

"God bless you, Will," she murmured to herself.

Conditions in steerage were gruesome. Overcrowded with inadequate, washing and eating facilities. The other passengers were mainly immigrant families, seeking a way out of the squalor and poverty they had known at home, crowded together, often sea- sick. The crying children, frayed tempers, and shear stench of unwashed bodies filled Will with both compassion and revulsion.

These people were desperate to build a new life. Many were farmworkers hoping to get an allotment of land and build a cabin on their own place.

Tom and Will took a break to smoke a cigarette on the deck. It was cold and blustery but a relief to be out of the crowd for a while.

"It's alright getting your homestead," Tom said, "but unless the government stops the big outfits grazing their herds on the land they give the people, they'll have a devil of a job hanging onto their places. The big guys will see them off. I reckon that's just as risky as prospecting, don't you, Will?"

"I don't know what to think," he replied. "Some will make it. We've got to make sure we do."

Up here on deck, Will's hopes were high again. Anyone travelling in the fug-hole called steerage was bound to be a downcast some of the time. But he was going to make it. Perhaps if the prospecting is good, he could get land and build a good farm. Penny would surely join him then.

One morning, after what seemed like an eternity at sea, they were awakened by the ship's horn blaring. Looking out, they saw the outline of the Statue of Liberty, that famous symbol of freedom. A cheer went up; they had arrived in New York. Tugs were attached to escort the ship into the harbour. Later, they disembarked and started the long process of going through immigration in the famous Ellis Island, where all newcomers were screened before being allowed into the country. A milling throng of people, with baggage and children, tired and bewildered, queued patiently amongst their belongings.

The immigration officers worked steadily through the queue. After a whole day of being unable to leave, Tom, Will, Philip, and their companions were at last able to tell an official that they would be crossing over to Canada, and as they were British subjects anyway, was it possible for them to be cleared and on their way? It was not, but eventually, halfway through the next day, they were seen, and their papers cleared. It was not the fault of the immigration authorities, just the sheer volume of people passing through.

"Phew, glad to get that over," Tom said, and they all agreed. Tomorrow, they would be off, bound for the gold fields.

"Must get this letter in the post," Tom added, "and let the folks know we have arrived this far."

"Yes, and I must get a letter to Penny," Will said; he was exhausted after the hassle of the last two days.

Back at the doctor's house, things were settling down to a pattern again. There was a new man to drive the doctor's carriage and a young maid to help with chores. Martha was now employed in a large house a short ride away. There the staff consisted of a cook, kitchen maid, general handyman, lady's maid, and butler. Penny would call in and see her sister on her afternoon off, and she was always made welcome in the kitchen. They were a happy bunch and had many laughs together.

Martha was courting David, a young man who worked the street market as a cheapjack, and he got up to some amazing antics to attract a crowd to buy his wares. A pet gag of his was to offer china items at a price; if no one came forward quickly, he would break them with his walking stick, smashing the lot, making as much noise as possible. It nearly always happened that when he held the next lot up, someone would put in a bid quickly, then others would follow.

"You've got to get the first bite," he explained. "Then it is easy. They all want what others have got."

Penny liked David; he was brash, but he thought the world of Martha and was very kind and considerate. "Have you heard from Will yet?" he asked.

"Just a short note to say they had arrived in New York. He said the journey out was awful; it must have been bad for the families. He said a lot of them were terribly sick. I do not, suppose I shall hear much for some time now. They have a very, long journey across Canada." Penny fell silent.

"I can't say I envy them. By all accounts, it is difficult terrain, freezing cold in winter."

"I know, David. I wish he had never gone, but he felt he had to try."

Penny wondered if refusing to marry him until they had more security had convinced Will to go. Or had it been Tom's vivid account of his adventures that made up his mind? It was too late now to regret her decision. He was gone and may never get back.

The days stretched into weeks, and no word came from Will. Penny threw herself into her work with renewed zeal. The doctor's wife was even frailer, and Penny's days were taken up with additional nursing tasks. Some three months on, the doctor's wife died quietly in her sleep. The doctor himself, now that he was on his own, seemed lost.

One day, he called Penny into his study and said, "I have decided to retire. I shall be putting the house up for sale and buying a small place by the sea. You would be welcome to continue as my housekeeper, but I shall not be able to keep the driver and maid on."

Penny was not surprised, but she did not really want to leave Martha and her friends. Before she could really come to a decision, she received an urgent letter from home. Jane, her younger sister, was desperately ill. It appeared she had taken a chill after getting a soaking whilst out on a picnic. But she had become feverish and developed a harsh cough. Now there was no doubt she was consumptive and fading fast.

The doctor was sympathetic; he said, "You must return to your parents straight away. Do not worry about me. I will manage."

The journey home was a sad one. She had not been back for some time. She hadn't liked to ask for time off when the doctor's wife was so ill. Now she was not looking forward to being home; the feeling of apprehension hung heavy on her. She trod the old route from the station down Havelock Road, along the front to George Street, hoping that the carrier was there.

"Hi there," a familiar voice called. It was the carrier. "I waited a while longer; I thought you'd be on the train."

Penny climbed gratefully up beside him. "Thanks," she said.

"Sad business, this," he said.

With a jerk on the reins, they moved off into the gathering dusk. Penny was so preoccupied with her thoughts that she hardly noticed the journey. When the horses pulled up at the gate of her parents' cottage, she was jolted out of her silence.

"Here we are," the carrier said. "I hope you find your sister improved." What could he say in such a situation?

Penny squeezed his hand and said, "Thanks."

Her mother met her at the door. "Oh, Penny," she cried and flung her arms round her daughter.

Penny hugged her mother and followed her back inside. Her father sat at the table; she thought he looked haggard and old.

"Hello, Dad."

He looked up and said, "Penny, my love; I'm glad you could come. She's asleep, so come and have a cup of tea and tell us all your news."

Penny pulled a chair up to the fire, and her mother set about making the tea.

Later, Penny went to see her sister. Jane looked exhausted and was fast asleep, her pallid face lit only by two feverish spots on her cheeks. During the night, the dry cough racked her frail body and wore her out. Penny sat pensively by her sister, now sleeping on the chaise longue in the front parlour.

There had never been consumption in the family before, and Penny knew there was little hope for Jane. She felt so helpless. Her sister had been about to marry Jason Tebbit, a young farmer from the next parish. It saddened her to see the anguish in the young man's face. They were so young and so in love.

Lizzie, their mother, remained cheerful despite it all, a brave little woman who kept everyone going.

CHAPTER 5

Out into the Unknown

❧ ❧ ❧

Bill Thompson was very quiet; he had seemed to gain a gentleness he had never had when they were children. During the week, Penny had little time to worry about herself, sharing with her mother the night nursing, sponging Jane's brow when she was feverish, changing her clothes, and keeping the room warm. If the temperature changed, the coughing would start. Gradually, Jane gained a little strength, and when the weather warmed, she was able to sit on the porch for a while.

Time went on, and still no word from Will; Penny's heart grew heavy. She felt sure he must have met with an accident, but she had no way of contacting him or the companions he had gone with. She did not even know where his parents lived. In fact, when she thought hard about it, she realised she knew little about his background. They had become so close to each other that nothing else had seemed important. She would have given anything to have been able to talk to someone else who knew Will and who might be in touch with him.

The doctor was pleased with Jane's progress but was worried that she could not stand another winter. Jason, frightened of losing her, mortgaged his farm and arranged for her to enter a sanatorium in Switzerland. Penny helped her mother collect clothes and toiletries together. They travelled to

London to see Jane and Jason off, as her young man was to escort her to the sanatorium.

None of the family could afford to visit her, but she wrote letters to them saying how much better she felt in the clear mountain air.

Penny stayed at home with her parents. They were delighted to have her company, even though she was rather quiet.

"You know, there is a sadness about Penny these days," Lizzie said one night. "I can see it in her eyes."

Bill Thompson nodded. He knew what his wife meant. He had seen that the careless feel of youth had deserted his daughter.

"You can only do your best to bring them up," he said. "You can't hope to save them from all the knocks of life."

"Well," his wife replied, "she is young; let us hope she gets over it. I expect she fell for some young man in London."

Martha came home for her summer holiday. Penny went to meet her train. She was so pleased to see her again. They had been such friends, and she had missed her companionship more than she realised. As the carrier's horses wound their way up the steep hill out of Hastings, the two girls sat in companionable silence, listening to the clip-clop of the horses' hooves on the hard road and the birds and animals preparing for sleep with a final song and a soft mooing. Perfume from the wild roses and honeysuckle rose to their nostrils, and they felt a sense of peace all around them.

"I love this kind of summer evening," Martha said. "What a treat it is to get out of London. Sometimes I feel like coming back home. But I would miss all the bustle. Don't you miss it, Penny?"

"Well, yes, but I did miss home, and with Jane away, I wanted to stay near the family for a bit." Penny dropped back into thought. Did she really want to stay here? She did not want to go away so soon. But there was time yet for making a decision.

Lizzie who had been listening for the carrier's cart, met her daughters at the door. While Martha gave her mother a hug, the carrier cheerfully handed down her cloth bag. "See you for the return journey, then?" he asked.

"Don't let's talk of that yet," replied Martha.

He laughed, waved his whip, and drove off.

"Come along in," Lizzie said. "The kettle has boiled. I expect you are ready for a nice cup of tea. See who is here, Father," she called out.

Bill Thompson found it difficult to show just how he felt. He was an undemonstrative person, but the warmth of his voice conveyed his real pleasure at having yet another of his daughter's home.

In the days that followed, the two girls went for many long walks down the lanes they had known so well as children. They called to see the miller and inquired after his sons. They had both gone into the army and were now serving in the Boer War under Kitchener. The old man was very, proud.

"They were at the surrender of Prinsloo," the miller boasted, "and then, they routed out the old devil De Wet. If Oliphant's Nek, hadn't been abandoned, they would have trapped him. But it will soon be over now. The main resistance has been broken. It's only guerrilla units continuing the war."

As they walked home, Martha turned to Penny and asked, "Why do you think the men always have to prove how brave they are, when we would rather have them safe at home with us?"

"I don't know. Maybe it's the spirit of adventure that they need to fulfil."

"David has volunteered for this war, you know."

"Oh, Martha, I am so sorry. I thought that you two would get married and settle down."

"He didn't think he was good enough for our family. 'What would your father say when he found out I was a street trader with little money and even less prospects?' he said.

"So now he is gone to try and, rise up, through the ranks, and then he says he will ask father for my hand. By the time he is an officer, I will be over the hill."

Penny started to laugh; the thought of Martha, so pretty and petite and young, being over the hill was ridiculous. Even Martha found it funny, and they turned into the cottage gateway, still laughing. Lizzie, hearing them, smiled. She thanked heaven to hear them in high spirits; they had been sad for too long.

Martha's holiday was flying by. They went on picnics by the sea at Pett-, Level, joyfully scrambling up Chick Hill to collect the pony and trap from the farm before setting off through Pett, and down Robin Hood Lane. It was a longish journey home, which they both enjoyed, chatting, singing, and gathering wildflowers. They hadn't had a holiday together since their school days; it was a brief recapturing of their childhood.

"Do you ever think about Will these days?" Martha broached the subject as the two of them were busy collecting their things for her return to London.

"Yes, but it hasn't seemed so bad since you came home."

"You should get out and socialise. I think you have to face the fact that he may never return, now."

"Don't say that, Martha. I can't believe I shall never see him again."

The next day, Martha left on the carrier's wagon; she waved until she was out of sight.

CHAPTER 6

Decision Time for Penny

B & B

The time had come for Penny to decide. She could either join the doctor as his housekeeper in Bognor, where he had retired (it was still in Sussex, but a good fifty miles from her parents' house). Or she could return to London in a new post. Finally, she decided to ask her mother for advice.

"I don't really want to return to London," she told her mother. "And I don't think I would like Bognor. I must get a job soon, but I'd like to stay near here. Really, I would like to get a job in one of the big houses."

"Well, if you're sure that's what you want, I could find out about the post of housekeeper at the hall. Mrs Griffin was saying the present one is leaving at the end of the month." Liza looked thoughtful. "But won't you miss all the bustle of town?"

"No. I feel I want a complete change; there is nothing there for me now."

"Would you like to tell me about it, Penny?"

Thankful to have a chance to unburden herself, Penny told her mother the whole story.

"Oh, my poor Penny. I think you are wise to have a change. It will be hard to pick up the pieces, but little by little, it will get less painful. And perhaps one day, you'll meet someone else you can be happy with."

A few days later, her father came into the kitchen where Penny was preparing dinner. "We shall miss having you to make the rabbit pies," he said, smiling. "But I think you will be alright. I'll take you to the hall this afternoon to see the mistress. Squire said if you were anything like your mother, they'd be only too pleased to have you."

"Oh, Father, you shouldn't have gone to all that bother for me."

"It wasn't for you, you, silly goose," he replied. "How much tongue pie would your mother give me if I didn't do what I was told?"

Penny laughed and said, "I'm sure she terrifies you."

Her mother came through the door at that moment; she got the gist of the conversation and said, "Wouldn't it be lovely, though? You'd be able to come and see us when you had a spare day off."

Seeing her mother standing there looking so pleased, Penny realised how hard it must have been for her parents, only seeing their children once a year. Now with Jane away, they would be even lonelier if she went away.

She gave her mother a hug and said, "I will be home like a shot whenever I get time off."

Penny was so excited but also nervous. The squire's wife had appeared rather haughty to her as a child. She hoped she would make a good impression and wondered if she would be able to cope with all the entertaining and catering if she got the job. Of course, she would not have to worry about the fruit and vegetables or flowers, for that matter. A good supply was grown by the head gardener and his team. She sat beside her father in the trap, wearing her Sunday best and feeling as if she was off on a new adventure.

"Don't be nervous," Father said. "They might be nobility, but they are nice folks for all that; you'll be alright."

They drove up to the property gate, and the gatehouse keeper came out and let them in; they continued down the long drive to the redbrick Manor House. Partially hung with tiles and festooned with roses, it had an attractive, mellow appearance.

The door opened as they drew up, and the squire came out. "Hello there, Thompson," he said jovially. "I see you've brought your gel, then. Come along in. My wife will join us shortly. Take a seat."

He ushered then into the front room. Easy chairs and a large settee were arranged on a beautiful Chinese carpet. There was a marble fireplace, over which hung a large rifle.

Seeing Penny looking at it, the squire said, "I used that gun for big game in India."

Now looking around, she could see other Indian items. A large wooden elephant held a brass tray aloft, and an inlaid box sat on the massive sideboard, along with decanters in their case.

Crossing to the sideboard, the squire said, "Care for a drink while we wait?"

Mr Thompson declined on behalf of them both; secretly, Penny thought a stiff drink might help her through her ordeal. The squire poured himself a brandy and sat down. Penny thought him a very pleasant person, and his welcoming manner made her feel less nervous. When his wife came in, she was dressed for tennis and looked flushed from her exertions.

"Phew, isn't it warm?" she exclaimed. "But lovely weather. I am glad you could come, Penny. We have heard a lot about you from the doctor. Did you know he is an old friend of my husband? They were at school together."

"What a coincidence," Penny said, surprised.

"Yes, isn't it? We won't need to take references for you. Your mother has helped us for years, and knowing how well our friend thought of you, we have no doubts in taking you on."

The squire's wife rang the bell, and the maid came in.

"Bring some tea and biscuits, please," she said. "After we have had tea, we'll show you around and let you see what the duties will involve. This is a larger house to run than the doctor's, with more catering to do for guests. But you'll find that hours are more regular than you've been used to."

Addressing Penny's father, she said, "You and your wife will be pleased to have Penny near home, especially with Jane away. How is she getting on in Switzerland?"

"She says she's much better but isn't strong enough to return home yet," Bill replied. "We are hopeful that it was caught in time. We've always been a healthy family; no one has had consumption before."

"There is so much of it about; perhaps she was a little low when she caught it."

They drank their tea, but Penny did not have a biscuit, afraid of making a mess. Still a little nervous, she caught the eye of the squire, whose eyes twinkled merrily at her.

"Come on," he said. "Come and see the gardens and glasshouses first; you'll be interested in them, Thompson."

"He is obsessed with those glass houses," his wife remarked, "but we will come and see them now. Do you think you could come in the morning, Penny? Then the housekeeper who is leaving can show you just what the job entails."

"That would be a great help. But do you think she will mind?"

"Not at all. She is only leaving us because her brother needs her to keep house for him now his health is poor."

"I will be here for nine, then," said Penny.

"Good; that's settled, then."

They went out into the garden, through the gate, into the walled kitchen garden. Pear, apple, peach, and nectarine trees were trained to the walls on espaliers. Flowers for cutting grew in front of the fruit trees, and in the middle was a large square where they grew vegetables. On the sunniest side grew the raspberries and strawberries and tucked away in the corner were two beehives.

"Careful," the squire called out. "You don't walk in their flight path."

"The bees are another of his hobbies," his wife told Penny.

"Do you help with them?" she asked.

"No chance," she replied. "They are far too hot for my liking. My hobbies are tennis and people. I love plenty of company."

The glass houses had that warm humid smell of the jungle; vines hung, festooned with grapes. Lilies gave off their pungent aroma in great profusion. It was like going into another world. Penny could understand the squire's enthusiasm for his greenhouses, for they were heated by hot water pipes, and many unusual plants prospered in this atmosphere. Gorgeous blooms, safe from the weather and pests, nestled on shelves near the hot pipes.

"Isn't it wonderful?" Penny exclaimed.

"Yes, it is rather," the squire said, looking pleased.

He liked to impress visitors with his plants. But Penny's amazement was so fresh and honest. It was apparent she had never seen anything like it before.

"Do you think you'll like it at the hall?"

Penny, who had been lost in her thoughts, was jolted back to reality by her father's question.

"Yes," she replied. "I think it will be a wonderful opportunity."

"Your mother will be pleased."

"What about you? Will you be pleased too?"

He laughed and said simply, "Never could understand you girls."

No, Penny reflected to herself; he never had understood how she felt. And in her early years, he had seemed so severe. She was sure he had given her mother a hard time with his moods. In his middle years, he seemed to have mellowed somewhat. Penny decided that men were very, different from women in the way they thought. Why was it, she pondered, that if women were talking, it was considered just chatting, but for men, it was considered serious debate? If her mother was quiet, she was sulking, but her father made the excuse that he was not in a mood, merely thinking. Life was very unfair for women, she decided. She would not have anything to do with men. She now had a good job and her independence. That was how she intended it to stay. Will had gone away; she tried not to think of him, as the pain was still with her. She had loved him dearly and thought he felt the same. Now she had a chance to start a new life with her own people. It gave her a feeling of belonging and a chance to renew the close bond with her mother.

Back at the cottage, Lizzie had the tea laid ready; she was at the door to greet them.

"How did it go, then?" she asked when they were barely inside. "Tell me all about it."

"Don't fuss, woman," Bill snapped. "Give us a chance to get in."

"Don't be so irritable, Father; Mother is only excited to know if I got the job." Then, smiling at her mother, Penny told her the good news.

"I am so pleased for you. And for me; it will be so lovely to have you near."

She was still excited, but her father smoked his pipe quietly; a man of few words, if he was excited, he certainly didn't show it.

Next morning, Penny was up early and ready to go to the hall. She was not sure how long it would take to walk, but it was a sunny morning. The birds were singing. and her spirits were high.

The housekeeper turned out to be friendly and went out of her way to make things easy for Penny. By the end of the month, when she was finally on her own, there was no aspect of her job that she had not been shown. Everyone made her very welcome, and she immediately felt at ease.

CHAPTER 7

Travels in the Wilderness

ß ♂ ß

Will, Tom, and their friends had been travelling for what seemed like an eternity. It was hot, and the mosquitoes were a constant threat. Each evening, they would make a brushwood fire in the hope that the smoke would drive them off. But there were always so many that got into the tents and whined around their heads, searching for a good meal.

A vast area stretched before them, and progress was slow. Wherever possible, they took to the rivers in their boat, making caches of supplies for the return journey and to lessen the load as they went. The trail was often blocked by dams made by the beavers.

"At least travelling in the heat," Will said, "we don't have to worry about wolves."

"No, you are right about that, but I won't be sorry when it cools off a bit."

Tom was fixing the boat, which had been badly damaged on an unexpected stretch of white water. This morning, they had met their first group of Indians; their villages were close to the river, and these shy people had many fish hanging out to dry.

"We should trade some stores with these people for furs," Tom said. "It will soon be too cold for ordinary clothes."

They managed to make the Indians understand, and they were as pleased with the stores as Will, Tom, and their friends were with the fur clothes. Anything must make a welcome change to all that dried fish; Will mentioned how awful it smelled.

"Don't knock it, Will. I expect we shall have to eat it too before this trip is over."

Will felt just a touch of apprehension. Was it possible that things might go wrong? No, he pushed the thought from his mind. He meant to get on and make his fortune, or at least enough for a small farm so he could go home and marry Penny.

The short summer was coming, to a close, and they knew that it would be winter when they arrived in the Rockies. Occasionally, they saw caches of stores placed by others on their way to the gold fields. Eventually, after many weeks of travelling, they reached the Rockies; it was awe inspiring.

"My God," Will said. "I never realised they were so high."

At the highest, they towered to above four thousand feet. Scrub and scree made the going even harder. Snow was beginning to cover the tracks, and they were constantly in fear of falling into a ravine. As they got higher, they had to rope the packs and hoist them up with axes. Their fingers and toes were numb, and the frost gathered on their breath. They intended to pick up the trail to Lake Telson, bypassing Skagway and making for the Chilkoot Pass. The river crossed the path many times, and they often had to wade across; they walked on and on. Uneven terrain played havoc with their feet. Tom's feet were too blistered to go on. It had been a terrible walk over miles of sharp stones, and everyone was in great pain with every step they took.

"I just want to lay down and rest," Tom said, groaning.

"You can't do that," Philip said. "We shall have to make camp if we want to keep the bears away."

Will set himself to light a fire and make a hot drink while the others set up camp. It had been a long day, for it was already twelve o'clock, but as light as noon. From where they were down in the river bottom, they could see a scrub fire which had been burning for some time. There were sounds like gunshots, and then a huge boulder split with heat and crashed down the mountainside. Thousands of feet to the left of the fire, a great waterfall cascaded down, caused by the melting snow and ice from glaciers above. A robin sat in a tree above the camp all night, no doubt fooled by the light of the fire. Night passed with no trouble from bears, kept at bay by the smell of fire. They were all surprised to find they were on the outskirts of Canyon City. So it was decided to find a bunkhouse and rest for a day before pushing on to Sheep Camp.

Next morning, everyone was in better spirits, and by eight o'clock, they set off for Sheep Camp, through heavy woods, along deep rocky and often bogey hillsides, broken by several deep gullies. The ascent was steep and slippery, with masses of fallen rock in places.

There was an aerial railway overhead, and it was a strange sight to look up and see a cook stove, a bale of hay, lumber, and other things flying by in baskets in mid-air. From Canyon City, these things were carried to the top of the pass, a distance of about nine miles.

"Just look at that," Tom said, pointing over the side of the track to where a horse had gone over. "He broke his back, poor old chap."

But that was only the first one. All along the line, beasts had gone over with their heavy loads. The stench was dreadful. Some had been shot to put them out of their misery. Even the dogs were carrying large loads.

The mountain was close on four thousand feet high, with an angle of 45 degrees, covered in deep snow, which during the day had become soft, freezing over again at night, making it difficult to get a foothold.

They finally reached the top; looking back, they could see the riverbed below them, now filled with ice and snow. On either side, mountain after mountain, snow clad and intermixed with peculiar-shaped glaciers.

"Thank God we have made it this far," Will said, shivering. "Just look how the weather has closed in."

The stillness and solitude of this icebound region oppressed him. Now that they were on the summit, it was bare of trees and bushes. The trail led through a narrow rocky gap, and the whole scene was one of complete desolation.

Descending was even more hazardous, as there were loose shattered rocks under the snow. The snow reflection was so painful to their eyes that they were obliged to rest more often. At long last, after wading through snow sometimes waist high, they came at last to Lake Lindemann.

"Thank goodness," Tom cried. "We shall be able to rest our feet now and go by boat."

Will looked at his feet, which were covered with the most broken blisters he had ever seen. His companions were in an equally bad state. They decided to rest up for a while. The bunkhouse here was a bit rough, but anywhere would have seemed like a palace in their exhausted state. Next day, they decided to reassemble their boat, which had been dismantled for the journey; this was quite a task, as it also had to be caulked.

Those who had built a boat or hired one at an exorbitant price looked at their boat with envy.

"We shall have to camp with the boat and have an all-night watch," said Tom. "Can't be too careful. Don't want her pinched while we sleep."

The others agreed.

Sure enough, on the second night, Will was on watch when he heard a small sound; knowing that he'd be overpowered on his own, he banged loudly on an empty can he had rigged up as a gong. Suddenly, all was confusion. Something heavy hit him on the back of his head; with an angry roar, he turned on his assailant. Tom and their little band of friends came tumbling out of the tent, armed with axes and shovels. This was more than the three desperate characters had bargained for, and they turned and made off into the night.

"Phew, that was a close one," Will said, rubbing his head ruefully.

"Yes, it is time we moved on. This place is too expensive. Folks are getting desperate for boats, just to get away before their cash runs out."

"You can say that again," Philip said.

Will liked Philip; tall and fair, the kind of lean frame of a permanently undernourished person, he was always cheerful and full of enthusiasm. He had been a farm labourer who was well skilled with timber. During the trip, it was he who had cut replacement parts for the boat. He had cut staves to help hump the load over rough ground. But in spite of his knowledge and kindness, there was just one worry. Was he strong enough to last the journey? Looking at his friend now, Will realised just how concerned he was for him. There was a gaunt look about his face. They had been through hell. It must get easier soon. Tom was a good leader and Will was glad to have the benefit of his brother's experience on this trip.

It had been a good thing to travel in a group of five. It was enough people to keep warm in the tent and useful when they had to defend themselves, as they had this time. And it meant they could carry the larger things, such as the boat, over difficult terrain.

Apart from Will, Tom, and Philip, there was Mike, an Irishman, and Callum, a Scot. Both had come from agricultural backgrounds. Mike's folks had become landless during the famine, and he had drifted over to England in search of work. Callum was that breed of Scot who had built many a nation. A born expatriate, stubborn and tenacious, it was he who urged the others on when he thought they were weakening. He and Mike would often break into song. Two Celts together, they were great pals.

They packed all their gear into the boat and set off in a stiff breeze, reaching the end of the lake, seven miles in all, in an hour. Here, the boat was unloaded onto wagons, while an expert crew took the boat through the rapids to Lake Bennett.

Tom and Philip went with the boat, while Will, Mike, and Callum accompanied the stores. The wind was bitterly cold, and it stayed with them, but by nightfall, they made camp in the brush. Everyone slept until around 5 a.m., when after a cooked breakfast, they set off again. Progress was slow now, as the wind had eased. Lake Bennett was at least twenty-six miles long: a pleasant interlude before the terrors of Lake Tagish.

"This is where things get difficult again," Tom said, giving them a rundown of what to expect on this next leg of the journey. "We shall come to a part known as Windy Arm, where many boats have been upset. The mountains on both sides open, up, and a wind is always blowing. It causes whitecaps on the water, sometimes making it necessary to lie to for days, watching and waiting for a chance to get through."

"If it's going to be that windy," Philip said, "hadn't we better tie everything down?" He began putting a belt around his jerkin and tying on his hat.

The others laughed.

"What about a bit of string to tie the paddle to your hand?" Mike quipped.

"You know, that might not be a bad idea," Tom said. "If we capsize, at least we'd have something to hang on to."

In the end, they tied a string to each paddle and tied it around their waists.

They set off cautiously. Before long, the wind got hold of the boat. With much creaking and shaking, they hit the white waters, hanging on for dear life, steadying the boat as best they could; drenched with freezing spray, they sped through, at times convinced they'd be pummelled to death by the sheer weight of the water.

Just as suddenly, it seemed they were through and entering a river with a swift current, which brought them into Lake Marsh. Hungry and tired, they set about making camp.

"Let's have a good rest tonight and make an early start in the morning."

Tom's suggestion was received with relief. Everyone was exhausted, not just by the exertion but also by the sheer stress of the day.

When they rose early the next morning, they found the wind gone and were obliged to row, each taking a turn with the oars. They proceeded with some anxiety, for at the end of Lake March, they had to pass through the Grand Canyon, a long wall of rock from fifty to a hundred feet high. Here the water dashed through at a tremendous pace. It was a miracle the boat was not wrecked trying to stop her at the end; as it was, Mike had a badly grazed knee, and everyone was buffeted and bruised, their clothes soaked through.

Once again, the boat had to be unloaded and everything carried to the White Horse Rapids. Tom decided they should get warm and dry (and have a good meal inside them) before pushing on.

The next morning, they reloaded the boat, and Tom spoke to them before boarding.

"If we do capsize," he said, "it could be hours before our next meal. No, we should not look on the black side of things. It's not for nothing that a lot of people know this placed by the name of Miners' Grave." He spoke very seriously. "Will and I will guide her through, and I want the rest of you to try and keep the stores from shifting and capsizing us."

They all nodded in agreement, for Tom and Will were undoubtedly the most experienced in the boat. Tom and Will stood in the front of the boat, hat and coat off; they worked like Trojans to keep it in the comb of the falls, each wielding his oar to fend off obstructions. With one bound, the boat flew over the rocks; with almost superhuman effort, they guided it into safe waters. The others sat in the boat, white with fright. Now that it was over, Will's legs felt weak, and his hands were trembling.

"My God," Mike shouted. "You both deserve a medal. I was petrified."

"Too damn true," added Callum.

Now that the tension was over, they all fell to talking and laughing at once. There were snags and rocks everywhere, as they passed the wooden crosses marking the spot where less lucky miners lay.

Having now entered Lake Le Barge, they decided to once more,to make camp, and many others also tied up here. There was game to shoot, and relief at surviving the rapids ran so high, it was almost a party atmosphere. It was good to sit around a fire, sharing the meat and having a good chinwag, until at last fatigue overcame them, and they rolled up in their blankets, drifting off into dreamless sleep. Everyone slept late, and they decided to stay one more day, to overhaul the boat and regain some more energy.

Callum and Mike set off to shoot some more fresh meat, while Will and Philip emptied the boat and turned her turtle, ready for recaulking. The day was fine, with a little more warmth in the sun. They had lost track of time, but it began to feel as if spring was stirring. There was a purple haze about the conifers, as if the sap was rising. The sun raised their spirits even more. Although the nights were still cold, the dry days made the going easier.

Will whistled as he prepared to caulk the boat. He had often felt he must have been mad to come on this escapade. But today, his optimism was high. What ice was still in the lake clung onto the edge and hung in canopies of icicles over the rocks. With the reflection of the sun, the wilderness seemed beautiful yet untamed.

The boat had suffered badly, and they had to spend another day nailing and then tarring the caulking before setting off again. But it was a welcome respite, and the two Celtic friends kept them in fresh meat and game, which helped to refresh and renew their energy. Poor Philip certainly needed this. His body reserves were not nearly as good as his companions. He looked just about all in. But after this two-day rest, he was anxious to get going. At first, it had been such a relief to stretch their limbs after spending so much time in the boat. But now, they were impatient to be on their way.

After they travelled a few miles, they realised how much time they had lost; presently, the snow and ice were all gone, and they entered a river and saw the first of the flowers on both banks.

A swift current carried them for about eight miles. Another boat, laden with stores, was ahead of them; suddenly, a rocky stretch of river appeared. The boat loaded with stores went to pieces on the rocks. Somehow, they missed it. Flying along, they passed wrecks on all sides. Some had saved their outfits and were drying them out on the banks. Others were trying to mend their boats. They called out, asking how Tom's party had missed the rocks. At last, they came to open water again.

There was just one more lot of rocks before the end of Thirty Mile River, and they hit it.

"Look out," they cried, too late to take evasive action; they hit the rock with a mighty thud. Fortunately, they had been travelling with such momentum that even with a large hole, the boat continued afloat until they got close to the bank.

Everything was soaked. But they were able to salvage most of their gear. Mike was the only one of the party to be hurt. He received a blow to the head which had caused a large swelling, and he appeared concussed.

Callum carried him to shore in a blanket. Then they all set about retrieving their provisions and gear from the river. The weather grew cold, and they kept a fire burning all night. For the next four days, they restored the boat and dried out their gear. Apart from a severe headache, Mike seemed none the worse for his ordeal.

Some of those who had called out to them as they passed on the way down now passed them, calling out, "Whose luck didn't hold out?" They waved as they went on their way.

Eventually, all was packed back into the boat. Mike, with his bruised head, was in the stern, wrapped in a blanket.

"You must keep warm with concussion," Tom said; he had been consulting his first aid book.

They set off once more. At the end of the Thirty Mile River, a Police Post asked,if they had lost anyone in the river. They had a long list of casualties, and the number of graves they had passed told the story.

At last, they reached the Big Salmon River. Will's spirits were high. Tonight, they would camp at Little Salmon, and the next stop was Selkirk, where he would be able to collect his mail and dispatch a letter to Penny. She was never far from his thoughts.

Little Salmon was a surprise, for at the junction with the Lewis River, there was a camp of about five hundred tents. Prospectors were busy panning for gold; only a few had any luck. But they decided to stay awhile and see if any of them could make a strike. After a week of solid work, the amount of dust they had was minute.

"I think we should push on to Dawson," Will told the others. "After all, we are wasting a good spell of weather to get a proper stake and settle before winter strikes again."

Tom agreed, for he knew the spring and summer would be short. Callum and Mike decided to stay. They had met up with some new companions, who were sure they were onto a lucky break. So, saying farewells and agreeing to meet up eventually in Dawson City, Tom, Will, and Philip set off for Selkirk.

Travelling seemed better with just the three of them. It was easier to move about in the boat, and being lighter, they made better headway. They were full of fun and optimism. Like Will, Philip had left a sweetheart at home. It had seemed to them both that the trip would be an opportunity to perhaps secure the money to make a better life for the families they both hoped to have, but both agreed they hadn't known how hard it would be.

Continuing, on to Fort Selkirk, they came to Five Finger Rapids, a bad piece of water to get their boat through. They were tossed about like a cork for what seemed an age, but in fact was only about three minutes; they manoeuvred the boat between the large rocks in a strong current, arriving on the other side wet but in one piece.

"Phew," Will said. "That was a close shave."

He felt a great relief. He would not be sorry to stop riding rapids in so small a boat.

As they journeyed on, they passed groups of prospectors digging by the riverside. Calling out, "Found anything yet?" they received the answer, "Just a little colour." No doubt, they were finding small quantities of dust, just as they had done at Little Salmon.

Arriving, at Selkirk, Will posted his letter to Penny. There was no mail for him, but he decided that Penny would have written to him at Dawson City. He was anxious to push on to get word from Penny and home. It had been many months now, and he was feeling somewhat homesick. Philip was also feeling homesick. Only Tom, who was fancy free, was not disappointed. He hardly ever wrote letters and did not expect to receive them. His mother would hear of this trip from Will. She no longer worried about him. He had been disappearing for long periods for years. But he always turned up again. Fortunately, she had a large family and not much time to dwell on it. He was considered wild by his family. But as a leader in an expedition, he was the best. Will thought highly of his elder brother.

While at Port Selkirk, they saw a cemetery where many settlers and Indians were buried following a great battle. Remembering those shy folks with whom they had traded for furs, Will was saddened by the sight.

After camping overnight, they began the journey to Dawson City.

Only one hundred and thirty miles to go. But the weather had deteriorated. The rain was lashing down with a strong wind against them, which meant they once again had to take to the oars.

They stopped at the mouth of Stuart River for a hot meal and a rest. Here there was another stampede of prospectors, and many caches of provisions in the trees in case of flood. Will and Tom built a brushwood fire while Philip prepared the meal. They were soon sitting around with a billy -can,full of broth, their clothes steaming in the heat. It had been a hard day battling against the wind and rain, but each day, they were getting closer.

"I wonder if the others did strike it rich," Philip said. "It didn't look very promising to me at Little Salmon. Plenty of people seem to have pushed on to Dawson. So that must be the place to be." He was still optimistic.

But Will was more concerned to get to Dawson for his mail. The gold could wait. A letter from Penny was what he needed right now.

"I think we should camp tonight," Tom said, "and make an early start tomorrow." He was already wrapping his blanket around him right there by the fire.

"Guess you're right," Will replied reluctantly, but Tom had closed his eyes and was already asleep.

Next morning, they were refreshed and warm. The rain had given up; everywhere was dripping and had that strange smell of rotting leaves and vegetation. The ground became noticeably boggier as they travelled on, but at last, they were within sight of Dawson City, in swampy ground at the foot of the mountain.

Boats were all along the shore, looking for a landing place. It looked a poor camping site; everywhere was waterlogged. They eventually found a spot on a rocky hillside, where they had to sleep in the soft places between the rocks. It was raining again, difficult to get a fire going to cook a meal and impossible to put up a tent.

Next day, after breakfast, they went to collect their mail and found a massive queue. Sorting seemed to be taking a long time. They were told it could be a week before they were able to collect it. Will's frustration and the constant wet made him miserable. The rain continued all week; shopping had to be done in the boat. Everything was extremely expensive: butter was $1.50 a pound, eggs were $3 per dozen. A licence to stake a claim cost ten dollars, and to record a claim, it cost fifteen.

Men often waited six weeks for a claim to be recorded; if it was likely to turn out rich, then the claim might not be granted. It began to look as if it was going to be hard to get past the system.

Penny had written, but Will was in a dilemma. She had said that the doctor's wife had died and that the house was up for sale, as the doctor was retiring. She also told him of Jane's illness, adding that she was returning to her folks to help care for her. But she had not enclosed the address. Will knew it was in Sussex but did not know where.

"We must move on, Will," Tom said. "We can't stay here. We shall soon have no money at all."

Tom knew Will was worried that if they moved on, Penny's letters would not reach him. But he believed they could find a stake somewhere else. Dawson was no place for a poor man.

CHAPTER 8

Penny at the Hall

$\mathcal{B} \, \mathcal{O} \, \mathcal{B}$

P enny soon settled in at the hall. But this was the first time she had organised such large parties. There were several local girls employed as maids, so she had plenty of help. Most of the entertaining was done at weekends, and tennis parties were held in the summer. The squire's wife had been an international tennis player before her marriage and still had a large circle of sporting friends.

Among the regular guests was John Cooper, a wealthy young farmer who found Penny very attractive. One day, he asked, "Would you like to come for a ride in the trap on your day off, young lady?"

"Penny is my name, sir," she replied, "and I'm not sure that I should accept an invitation from a guest."

The squire, overhearing this conversation, said, "You go and enjoy yourself, Penny; we don't look on you as a servant here. John will take good care of you." He smiled at them both. "Do you good, Penny; put the roses back in those cheeks."

Penny flushed and said, "Alright then, next Wednesday afternoon."

"'Good," replied John. "That's settled."

He moved off, mixing with the other guests. Penny watched him go, feeling somewhat uneasy. She hadn't been out with anyone since Will.

Hadn't wanted to. She had to face the fact that life had to go on. She couldn't brood about what might have been forever. John was a dark, handsome man with a cheeky smile. He looked as if he could be fun. It had been a long time since Penny had enjoyed herself. *Maybe things are looking up, after all,* she said to herself.

When Penny told her mother, Liza looked worried.

"Did you know when Jason Tebbit mortgaged his farm to send Jane to Switzerland, it was to John Cooper that he went?"

"No, I didn't know that; does it make a difference?"

"Well, up until two years ago, he was nothing. He was a rabbit catcher and a gambler. He won his farm at cards, they say. No one ever dreamed the stakes would be so high. But week after week, a small crowd of them played cards into the night. One farmer, carried away by the size of the stakes, got so into debt that the only way he could pay was to part with his farm; it seems a wicked way to get on in the world."

"Don't worry," she said. "I am not serious about him. He is just fun to be with."

During the months that followed, John took Penny dancing and to the races. She met lots of people and really enjoyed the company. John was very attentive and showered her with flowers and boxes of chocolates.

"Young John Cooper has really put the colour back into our Penny's cheeks," Bill Thompson said to his wife one day. "She could do worse. You suppose she could be a good influence on him?"

"I sincerely hope so," Liza said. "They do say he is farming very well, so perhaps the past is behind him."

The months went by, but Penny still insisted they were only good friends. At Christmas, he bought her a beautiful fur muff and a warm shawl.

"Now then, John, you shouldn't buy Penny such expensive presents when you are only friends," Liza scolded.

He flushed and said, "I would like to be more than a friend. But I am afraid if I ask her, I might lose her altogether; for some reason, I can't get her to take me seriously."

"Give her time. You are both young. Marriage is a serious business; you'd find it hard to be a good husband. Those cards would have to stop. No bride would want to spend night after night on her own."

There. It had at last been spoken of. Penny's mother always called a spade a spade. But John had never expected her to be so abrupt. He could see by her expression she did not approve of him. He looked hurt.

"It wouldn't be like that, I promise. I love her dearly. I would do whatever she wanted. I would be the happiest man alive, if only she would have me."

Penny realised that John had become very fond of her. She liked him, and he was fun to be with. But would she be happy if she married him? Common sense told her, here was a chance to marry well, to be mistress of her own house. It was no, any good thinking, if only. Will was not, going to come back now and claim her for his bride. That was all in the past; she must get on with living, even if a corner of her heart still ached. When at last he asked for her hand, she accepted. His delight was so great, he did not even notice her hesitation.

The wedding plans were made, and Penny became busy preparing the farmhouse, renewing the curtains, and changing the decorations, adding a woman's touch to what had been a bachelor establishment. She had so many plans.

"Isn't all this a bit expensive?" her father asked one day. "After all, farming isn't doing that well. Are you sure John can afford it?"

"Of course, he can," Penny replied, laughing. "He would surely have told me if he couldn't."

Nevertheless, Penny felt a touch uneasy. She had spent a lot of money, she knew, and she didn't really know just how well off, John was.

When next they were on their own, Penny asked John outright if he could really afford all the alterations she was having done in the house. His reply was, "You do whatever pleases you. I will find the money, never fear."

She breathed a sigh of relief. The fears voiced by her father had worried her more than she cared to admit. That worry out of the way, she pressed on with her improvements. And the house looked a treat. The furniture was all freshly covered with scattered cushions Penny had made herself. All the doors sported a new coat of paint. The beds had new chintz covers and curtains to match. And they were to have a maid to help with the work in the house and dairy. Penny had never worked in a dairy, separating cream and churning the butter. John had showed her how to do these things.

"You must know how to do the job yourself," he explained. "Otherwise, you won't know if your maid is doing a good job."

Penny was so happy. The invitations were ready to go out, and her dress was nearly finished; only that day, she had had the last fitting. She was singing as she went to call on her parents. As she passed the parlour window, they were deep in conversation; they looked worried.

Popping her head round the door, she called out, "Everything alright?"

"Nothing for you to worry about," Liza said. "It's Jane. She is coming home because Jason can no longer afford the sanatorium fees."

"Oh dear, has Jason had a bad year?" Penny asked.

Her mother replied, "And on top of that, he has to redeem the mortgage."

Penny couldn't believe it. She left the house immediately. There must be some explanation. John would tell her why he was calling in the loan. She hoped it was not because of her extravagances. After all, he would surely have said.

After hurrying home, she was out of breath and hot when she heard his voice: "Hello, over here."

He was working in the yard, mending the wheel on his trap, where the iron rim had worked loose.

"My word, you look flushed," he said. "What's up?"

"Jane is coming home."

"Well, that is good news," he said, smiling at her.

She bit her lip. "They are saying Jason can't pay the fees because you are recalling the loan. Tell me that isn't true." She looked at him with eyes brimming with tears.

"I have to," he replied. "If I don't, I shall lose this place. I need the money."

"Oh, John, why? Why let me spend when you could not afford it? I would have understood. Now how can I face my sister? They've lost everything because of me." The tears brimmed over.

"You worry too much about others," he replied stiffly. "They will find a way, just as I did."

"How can you be so callous?" Tears welled up again as she struggled to get her glove off. She tore his ring off and tossed it at him. "I can't marry you now." Turning on her heels, she set off back to her parents' cottage.

John just stood there for a moment. He had always taken just what he wanted out of life, without giving a thought to anyone else. Now he had lost the one person he really cared for. He wanted to go after her. He knelt in the straw, looking for the ring. But it was lost, as surely as his sweetheart. He began to cry, something he had not done since his boyhood days.

Penny began to write to all the guests to tell them the wedding was off.

"I only posted the invitations today," Lizzie said. "Won't you reconsider, Penny? Jane is a lot better now, and your father says Jason can work with him and take on the smallholding when we give up. They will be able to make a living, just as we have done."

"No. I realise now that John is a totally ruthless man. And I will never be able to love him again."

"He loves you, though. Think how he must feel."

"He hasn't got feelings. Family doesn't matter to him; he is hard, and I no longer want to share my life with him."

Penny went home less often now. She told herself they did not need her company so much, now that Jane was home again. But in her heart, she knew it was because she could not bear to see her mother so distressed. She had so looked forward to having her family settled near her, to be able to see the grandchildren growing up around her, to enjoy that close family relationship. She, Penny, had wrecked all these dreams. Once again, she had failed them, the parents who loved her so.

Everywhere she looked, she saw reproach in the eyes of those around her. She saw it especially in the eyes of the squire, who had no son of his own and had taken John Cooper under his wing, giving him help and advice with his farm. He missed the young man's visits to the hall, for most of the guests were his wife's friends. It was not that he was an unsociable man, but his interests were in the countryside, and in John, he had a kindred spirit.

Unable to bear his own company and not wanting his old friends to pity him, John Cooper took to travelling into town, where he visited tavern after tavern, playing cards, drinking a great deal, and losing heavily on gambling with dice. Then, singing and shouting, loudly, he would make his way home, or more correctly, his old horse who knew the way would take him there.

Penny would hear him through the open window. It made her sad to think she had caused his downfall. But she realised she had been about to marry more for position than love, and the knowledge made her feel ashamed. She had never felt for John what she had felt for Will. She had liked and enjoyed his company. But she was not able to confide this to her mother. She would have been shocked. People just did not talk about these things. Perhaps, Penny reflected, nice people did not have such immoral thoughts.

Now that everything had come to a grinding halt, Penny knew she would have to think carefully about what to do next.

Whenever she had time on her afternoons off, she took to walking in the fields and woods. The peace and solitude calmed her nerves, and she began to think what she should do. She had lost Will; nothing was ever going to be quite the same again. Now she had caused pain to her parents and probably brought about the ruin of John Cooper. Perhaps it had been a mistake to return home after so long. Her childhood friends had married and had children of their own. She had been so determined to show everyone that she could be a success. In her small way, she had been. But it was nothing compared to the grief she had caused. Could it be that success was not what she had thought, to secure a good job and make her parents proud; she knew now that to them, success would have been to be happy and make others happy.

Penny was restless. Once again, she knew she must leave; she had a feeling she would never return to live in her beloved Sussex. In a sense, she was taking leave of all her old haunts, storing in her mind the memory of how everything looked. The neat little cottages and villages, the oast houses and farms, the windmill, the winding river, the marshes with remote cries of curlews, and above all, the sea, with its rock pools containing their own small world of sea anemones, starfish, crabs, shrimps, mussels, and occasionally the poisonous weaver fish. She shut her eyes, listening to the soft surf. She did not want to leave, yet she could not stay. Part of her would always long for this place, but she would never again belong here.

Her mind was made up. She returned to the hall; without hesitating, she requested to see the squire and his wife. The tension in the room could have been cut with a knife. Penny offered her resignation, and they accepted it readily; they did not try to dissuade her.

"We are prepared to give you a good reference as a housekeeper," the squire said, "even though we deplore the way you ill-used our young friend." He was flushed with embarrassment but felt he had to say something.

"I am truly sorry for what I've done to John," Penny replied. "But perhaps with my leaving the district, it will save him some pain."

She felt like a child being disciplined. These people had been good to her. But they were John's friends, and she could not,expect them to understand her point of view.

"We would like you to pack your bags and leave today. This has been a painful time for us all. The sooner it is all over, the better."

The squire was obviously uncomfortable. He was by nature a kindly man.

His wife, who all this time had kept quiet, now spoke.

"Penny, I bear you no ill-will. You must have had a reason for turning John down. But I fear you may have turned away the chance of a secure home and plenty. I would like to wish you well. Goodbye then."

She shook Penny's hand, turned, and left the room, obviously upset, for she and Penny had got on well together. Penny bade the squire goodbye and went to her room to pack.

It did not take long to put her few possessions into her cloth bag. She left quietly by the back stairs, going through the kitchen garden and slipping out the back gate, soon heading down the lane to her parents' cottage.

They were working on their plot of land. Penny knew her mother had seen her. She had seen her look up from the row she was hoeing. But no one came to the cottage for some time. While she waited, Penny had a cup of tea and went over things in her mind. She had to tell them she was going. They would have to live with what she had done. She would go into exile to rebuild her life. Now there would be no grandchildren at the farm down the road, no Penny to pop in on her way to the grocer's. Just the weekly letter and, if finances allowed, a yearly visit to see them for a day or two. In the village, her mother would be known as "Mrs Thompson, whose daughter jilted John Cooper."

Eventually, her mother came in and said, "Make a cup of tea while I get washed up, Penny."

Her mother sounded cheerful, but she had puffy eyes, which showed she had been crying. She was going to put a brave face on it. Her father equally cheerful when he came in. Penny was grateful. They were not going to make it hard for her. She had dreaded this moment. She had not wanted to face Jane and Jason, either. She felt responsible for their misfortune, although she knew they did not hold anything against her.

As if reading her thoughts, her mother said, "Don't rush away too soon."

"Let her do as she wishes, Lizzie; she knows there is always home to come back to."

Penny smiled her gratitude to her father. If she was, to go, it must be soon, whilst her resolve was strong.

She wrote a letter to Martha, who had been coming home shortly for the wedding, and was pleased to get a long and understanding letter back. She wrote that she was shortly leaving her position to become a trainee nurse at the Nightingale Training School for Nurses. This training establishment, attached to St Thomas' Hospital in London, had been founded by Florence Nightingale with the fifty thousand pounds she had won as a testimonial for her work in the Crimean War, where she had worked relentlessly to relieve the suffering of wounded soldiers.

Martha wrote that she was very, excited to be able to train as a nurse and hoped to meet the great lady herself, as she had often looked in to see what progress students were making. In the meantime, wedding or not, Martha was coming home for a few days with the family.

Penny read the letter to her mother as she prepared tea.

"Florence Nightingale must be a marvellous woman to take such an interest in the school," Liza said. "After all, she must be in her seventies now."

Lizzie was very proud to have a daughter about to train as a nurse.

Penny wondered what had made her sister decide to try for a career; she had seemed such a homebody. Now she was full of enthusiasm for a new way of life.

Penny was delighted to see her sister again. When they were preparing for bed, Martha said, "If you haven't made up your mind what you want to do, why not consider coming with me?"

Penny did not reply for a moment; the question had taken her by surprise. But she had to admit she had felt a tinge of envy when she had read her sister's letter. She badly, needed to build a new life.

"Do you think I would make a good nurse?" she asked.

"Why not? You proved yourself very capable at the doctor's house."

Penny went to the bureau, sat down, and put pen to paper and wrote to the matron of the nursing school. She posted it next morning and then forgot about it in the busy days that followed. Martha was, as usual, full of fun, and they enjoyed long rambles. They borrowed the trap and took their mother for rides and even took Jane, who was now stronger, out for a day at the sea. They went along the coast to Winchelsea, with the carrier to transport them and their picnic, for Jane still tired easily.

Two days before Martha was to return to London, a letter arrived. It was from the matron of the nurses training school. She wrote that she was impressed with Penny's application and had received a favourable report from the doctor. She was invited for an interview and, if suitable, could start with the next intake of trainees.

It was with some trepidation that Penny attended her interview, carried out by members of the hospital board and the matron. But to her relief, she was accepted. She and Martha were to train together, living at the nurses' home for the next three years.

Returning to their parents' home to prepare to leave yet again was painful. But her mother, father, and Jane were very, kind and did not reproach her. Penny regretted that she did not feel as close to Jane as she did to Martha. She had been away so much. Jane had only been a schoolgirl then. Jason Tebbit called every day to see Jane and was friendly to Penny too.

Why don't you hate me? Penny asked herself. But they did not seem to feel any ill will towards Penny.

At last came the day when she must travel to London. The whole family waved goodbye. Penny waved to them all, but her view of the figures she left behind was blurred by her tears. Once again, she was off on a great adventure. This time, there would be no return.

CHAPTER 9

London Again

B & B

Jason Tebbit and Jane were married quietly in the little village church. Penny, still consumed with guilt, did not go. Fortunately, she was able to say, truthfully, that she was on duty. The couple were to make their home in a tiny farm cottage belonging to Jason's uncle. Jane was still far from strong but nevertheless happy to marry the man who had sacrificed everything for her.

Martha went down to her parents' home, taking Stuart to meet his future in-laws and to attend the wedding. When next Penny saw her, she was so excited.

"Honestly, Penny, Jane was a lovely bride, so pale and transparent with all that white lace. And what news I have, to tell you. John Cooper is married."

"Married! Who to?"

"Sarah Dugdale. Her father has a large farm in Rye."

The news startled Penny. How soon he had got over his distress. She felt guilty that she had left but was glad for him.

"I do hope he is happy, Martha." She looked so solemn that Martha laughed.

"Don't you want to hear my other news?" she asked.

"Yes, of course."

"Stuart and I have fixed a date; we are to be married in September."

"That is great news. I am so happy for you." Penny gave her sister a big hug and added, "I am glad you won't be far away; I shall miss you."

After Martha left, Penny sat thinking and remembering all that had happened since Will had gone away. Something must have happened to him. She had written to him at Dawson City. Had he never made it that far? Who could tell; she had told him she was returning, home.

Then, the awful truth dawned on her: He did not know where her parents lived. *Oh, Penny! You little fool.* By the time his letters arrived at the doctor's house, everyone who knew her would have gone, and the new owners would not know who she was. But what was the good of thinking of this now? Five long years had gone by. She had nearly married John. Will was probably married by now, anyway. All her heartaches had been self-inflicted, but that was no consolation. She would have given anything for a chance to put things right.

"Oh, well, you can't turn the clock back now, my girl," her mother would have said.

Penny realised how desperately lonely she was now that Martha spent so much time with Stuart. It would be worse when they were married. She tried to think logically.

You still have plenty of friends, so how can you be lonely? she asked herself. But even as she said it, she knew the answer. She was homesick. She had no roots in London, nothing to hang on to. She longed to be able to share the confidence of her mother, as she had when she worked at the hall. Then, she had been able to pop in and have a chat with her parents, and she lived among people she knew and who knew her and her family. She had burned her boats. Now, she was a refugee in a large city. Her heart was still in her beloved Sussex. She decided to return for Martha's wedding next September. As the months passed, the thought of returning home sustained her, and she became less unhappy. After her sister's special day came and went, however, her dissatisfaction returned.

It was a dull damp day, the kind of day when the clouds seem to hang on the buildings. Penny's spirits were as low as the clouds. She felt tired, isolated, and alone.

Going home for Martha's wedding had not helped. It had all been so unsettling, for as a bridesmaid, she had to be the very essence of cheerfulness. Her parents were pleased to see her, and they never mentioned John.

Jane and Jason had also been very welcoming, but in her heart, she bitterly reproached herself for their misfortune. They were obviously poor. Jane looked smart in her dress, which she had worked over by adding a new ribbon or two. Jason's suit had been pressed but was threadbare. The material had lost any body it ever had. They had a child now, a pale, wane little boy with no roses in his cheeks, only the pale transparency of his mother.

How could she feel anything but guilt when she saw them? She had caused Jason to lose his farm. Without her extravagance, John may never have called in the loan. But all that was behind her now. No amount of remorse could change things one jot. She must stop feeling sorry for herself. But she was so lonely.

Penny shivered. Leaves were turning on the trees. Life was very much like the seasons, she reflected. The spring flushed with promise, the warmth of summer in her love for Will. Was she now to be blown about by the autumn gales, to end up bitter and dried up, like the leaves in winter? So ran her melancholy thoughts as she walked through the park.

This won't do, she told herself. *Be grateful you have your health and a job you enjoy.* Determined to shake off her mood, she carried on back to the nurses,home, determined to stop moping and do something positive.

As she entered the hallway, she heard a familiar voice say, "I've been waiting an hour for you." Martha continued, "I was just about to give up. If you are, off for the rest of the day, we wondered if you'd like to come to dinner tonight?"

"Oh yes, please," Penny replied. "How could you have known I needed some good company to cheer me up? Are there any other guests coming?" She was happier already.

"Yes, we are having a house, warming. Just a few of Stuart's friends, his mum and dad, and then any of the nurses who are not on duty. You'll have to bring some cake back for the ones who can't come."

It was a wonderful evening. Good conversations over the meal with Stuart's parents, Martha, and Stuart, and a great deal of fun and laughter when the others arrived. Martha had made a tasty punch, and there were plenty of snacks. As the evening wore on, more and more people popped in and out of the small house; freshly decorated and with a good coal fire flickering away, it was very cosy and welcoming. The neighbours had all been invited in for a drink, and as Penny left with others from the nurses' home, there were calls of, "Goodnight and sweet dreams."

The cab drew away, with much waving and calling out; it was a night to remember. Penny slept well, untroubled by the remorse she had felt in the afternoon.

The following morning, she was back on the wards, bright as a button. The weather had lifted, and the sun was shining, not with any great warmth, but enough to keep spirits high.

Stuart's role as a junior partner was a busy one, for many of his patients in this working-class area worked on the wharfs as lightermen; others were porters in the Borough Market, moving huge consignments of fruit and vegetables in the early hours of the morning, for these perishable items had to get from the wholesalers to the shops the same day. Inevitably, accidents happened; in fact, many occurred: barrows slipped on wet cobbles, and lightermen often slipped between two vessels. Over the bridge, porters from Billingsgate rushed through the streets with baskets of fish balanced on their heads. The mess made the cobbles quite slippery, and this occasionally led to someone cracking their head on the slimy cobbles.

Stuart was up at dawn to deal with these calamities, then on to morning surgery, followed by his rounds, home for a bite to eat, and then on to the crowded evening surgery. Martha seldom saw him in the evening, and Penny often dropped round to keep her sister company.

"We shan't stay here too long," Martha said one night while pouring the tea. "Stuart says it is good experience, but when we have saved enough capital, we shall move to the country. I wouldn't want to raise a family here."

Penny agreed, saying, "It must be very difficult for the wives of lightermen; they have so many children, and with the men being taken on for day work, they can never be sure their household expenses will be met."

"It is even worse for the wives of Billingsgate porters; those pubs are open all day, and some men drink away their pay before they get home."

"Don't they look funny in those white smocks and hard hats over at the fish market?" Penny said. "I saw one porter with a basket of fish on his head, and some of the barrows have enormous loads, so perhaps it's thirsty work."

Martha laughed and replied, "It's smelly. That's a fact."

Sometime later, Martha was on an errand to deliver some linctus to an elderly patient in Blackfriars Road and decided to take a short detour up the Cut, as it is known. As she passed a pawnbroker, she saw a cart pull away in the traffic. The back of the young man driving looked vaguely familiar. Martha had only met Will on a few occasions, and she couldn't be absolutely sure, but it looked like him. If it was him, why would he be visiting the pawnbroker? It certainly did not look as if he had made his fortune.

Martha decided not to tell anyone but to come this way again on Monday to see if he would come back to redeem whatever it was. But although she waited about for a long time, he did not appear. After this, it seemed to Martha that wherever she went, she would see this elusive figure but was always unable to get near enough to hail him.

On one occasion, she called out, "Will!" But when the young man turned around, it was not him. "I am ever so sorry," she said. "I thought you were someone else."

"Won't I do then?" the young man asked, laughing. "I am as good a man as you'll find around here."

"Cor blimey, miss; he is real hot stuff," his tittering friend said. "The real McCoy."

Martha blushed and murmured, "My mistake; sorry."

They went off down the road, laughing.

This encounter rather unnerved Martha, so she decided she had better speak to Stuart and tell him what happened.

"Stuart, I am worried about Penny; she loved Will, and now she has nobody."

Stuart smiled and said, "Don't worry; she's happy in her work. You must stop trying to find her a husband; perhaps she doesn't even want to get married."

"She wanted to marry Will, only they lost touch." She looked thoughtful for a moment and then said, "I think I saw him coming out of the pawnbrokers in the Cut."

At this, Stuart laughed out loud and cried, "Good heavens, he doesn't sound much of a catch."

When Martha told him how she had tried to find him again Stuart look worried and warned her, "Do not do that again, Martha. I don't,want you approaching strangers like that. It could be very, dangerous; you might be followed and assaulted. Give me his name; I will make enquiries to see if anyone knows him around here, but it seems very unlikely."

Although he asked around, no one seemed to know Will Long.

Martha did not tell Penny about her escapades. She and Stuart decided it would be cruel to raise her hopes. Not only that, if it were Will, he may well have a wife and family by now.

Penny had changed jobs and was now at Guy's Hospital. She found this part of London very stimulating, for there was always so much going on and so many things to see. Especially on the river, with its constant traffic of boats and lighters, barges, and tugs. The people were friendly and passed the time of day with her as much as if she were in a village back home. She loved all the hustle and the smell of fruit and vegetables as she passed the market.

Porters rushed to and fro with their gaily painted barrows heavily laden, and horses and carts jostled for the best loading positions. The Cockney drivers exchanged good-natured ribald remarks.

Sometimes, there was a small band playing in the yard of the Mermaid Inn; the pearly king and queen would be collecting pennies for charity, mainly to help accident victims or families where there was an illness. Penny loved to join in the sing-along, that usually ensued. They sang all the well-known musical songs. Penny had a good voice; she had had plenty of practice singing in chapel as a child. But now, she smiled to herself as she wondered what her father would make of this. He would not approve, she knew. But she saw no harm in it. It was a pleasant happy time they were all having. It was said that this yard was the site of William Shakespeare's Globe Theatre. But Penny was sure the many friends she was with enjoyed their singalongs better than they would have enjoyed the Bard's plays.

One night, they were singing "Clementine," and the yard was packed with people. Suddenly, Penny felt her heart stop beating; there it was again: that unmistakable baritone voice. It could only be a ghost from the past, or someone who sounded like Will.

The dusk was falling, and it was difficult to make out features in the half-light. Penny pushed away towards the back, listening hard, but she couldn't find the voice.

In desperation, she called, "Will Long! Are you there?"

"Over here," a voice replied. "Is that you, Penny?"

The crowds drew back to let her through. It did not feel real, more like a strange dream. She stood in front of Will. He was with a slightly built woman of about her own age.

Oh, heavens; he is married, and I have blundered into his life again, was Penny's first thought.

Will could hardly speak; tears of joy ran down his cheeks.

"I thought I had lost you forever," he said gruffly.

"So, did I," Penny replied.

The woman with him touched his arm and said, "Aren't you going to introduce us, then?"

"Sorry, Sally. I didn't mean to be rude." Will turned and said, "This is Penny Thompson; Penny, my sister Sally."

"Pleased to meet you, Sally," Penny said.

"What are you doing here?" Will asked.

"I am a nurse at Guy's Hospital. What about you?"

"I am doing haulage and staying with Sally and her husband Andrew until I can get a place of my own."

"When I saw you with Sally, I thought perhaps you were married."

Will's face clouded and he murmured, "That's a different story."

She wished she hadn't said anything; it was a long time ago when they had fallen in love. She didn't know how he'd feel towards her now. Perhaps they had both changed too much for them to pick up their relationship again. But she was glad to know that at least he had not perished somewhere on the journey to the gold fields. She felt that Sally was a trifle cool towards her but told herself that was only natural. She probably felt her brother had been badly used.

"I must go," she said lightly. "I am on duty in half an hour."

"Can I walk you back?" Will asked.

"No, I wouldn't dream of it, but perhaps we could meet for a chat sometime."

"I'm not letting you get away again," Will said, smiling. "Meet me here tomorrow; what time do you finish?"

"Eight o'clock in the morning, but then I shall need some shut-eye."

"How about meeting here, then, at about 12:30? We could have a spot of lunch and a nice long afternoon."

"Lovely. See you then. Sally, I'm pleased to have met you."

Penny made her way back to the hospital. She just could not believe what had happened to her today. All those years, she had wondered what had happened to him. Now to suddenly to find him just down the road from where she was living and working; it was the most amazing coincidence. But then she asked herself, it may be Will, but was this the same Will? He had an air of sadness about him, indeed an air of maturity, as people sometimes do when they have had some knocks in life. It may be that the long separation had left them poles apart; she must accept that they may have nothing left in common. But even so, she found herself singing as she prepared for duty.

Some of the patients noticed; one old man said, "I think you must be in love."

She blushed, tossed her hair, and said, "Where did you get that idea from?"

But he only shook his head and smiled.

I won't tell Martha yet, she thought. *I'll wait and see how tomorrow goes.*

But her duties soon took, all of her attention. Tomorrow must wait.

"Say," Will asked Sally sharply, "what you are thinking?"

"I was just wondering, how are you going to explain the child to her?"

"I shall tell her the truth."

"Then be prepared to be rejected, because she won't want you after she finds out you weren't faithful to her."

"Damn it, Sally, I hadn't heard from her for two years when I met Naspa, and I'm not ashamed of the child; he is mine, and I love him and care for him."

"He is still a little half-caste. That will cause you trouble if you want to marry."

"Well, I'm not about to ditch the boy, anyway. If I marry, he must be part of my family; there is no way it will be any different."

Will fell silent. His sister could be right, but he also knew that she did not want him to leave. The money he paid her helped to keep her head above water. Andrew was a sick man and often unable to work, and the arrangement where Sally minded Will's son and he contributed to the family's upkeep worked well for them both. He could not have foreseen that he would meet Penny again. He had certainly not thought of ever marrying again after Naspa died. Even now, he felt responsible for what had happened. He had been overwhelmed by her beauty and kindness. She had come into his life when he was lonely. Now she was gone, leaving him to bring up their son.

Will tiptoed into to peep at the sleeping child. So angelic with his jet, black hair and long eyelashes, a small human dynamo in repose. Will looked at him and said fondly, "I won't let you down, Tim; not if I can help it."

CHAPTER 10

The Travelled Man Meets the Family

ß ℰ ß

Next morning, Will was up early; he had a removal to do just locally. He must not run over time today; he didn't want to keep Penny waiting. The job did not take long, and as he was returning, he saw his sister carrying the shopping home.

"Want a lift, then?" He leaned down and took the bags from her.

"No hard feelings this morning?" Sally said.

"No, it may not work anyway; it's been years since we were together." He flicked the reins and called, "Gee up."

They trotted up Union Street towards her little terrace cottage, which was in Great Street just off the Cut. Will dropped his sister off at the door and made his way to the stables. As he bedded the horses down, he could not help reflecting on what Sally had said last night. But he could not have left the boy behind. He probably had been wrong to comfort himself with an Indian girl. But he had loved her, and when she died, he had grieved. Maybe the boy was half-native, but he was his son, and anyway, wasn't he also considered something of an outcast in some quarters? Didn't it depend on prejudice on how people viewed these situations? He could only hope for understanding, nothing more.

When Penny came off duty, she hurried home and went straight to bed, setting the alarm for 11:30, to, be in plenty of time to meet Will. But she need not have bothered, for her thoughts would not let her sleep. Her mind went back over the events of the previous evening. It seemed so amazing that they should have met like that after all this time.

And when she mentioned that she thought him married, he had replied, "That's another story." Perhaps he was separated or a widower. Enough, for the present, it was sufficient that she had found him again.

Then she started to worry; she wondered, "How can I tell him about John, and what about Jane and Jason? How can I tell him I'm the reason they live in poverty?" Her feelings of guilt were overwhelming, until at last she got up and made herself a cup of tea. *It isn't any good,* she reflected; *he won't even want to know you when he realises what a bad lot you are.*

Will was exceedingly angry. Sally had heard him arranging to meet Penny, so why had she popped his suit in at the pawnbroker's again?

"You knew I wanted it today," he shouted at her. "It isn't as if I haven't given you any money; you can't have been short."

"You're making a fool of yourself, Will. She won't want you when she knows."

"Let her be the one to decide that."

"You know it isn't just the boy? Does she know about our gypsy blood? Does she know our mother is a full-blown Romany?"

Sally definitely liked hitting below the belt, but of course it was true. He wasn't surprised that his father had married the beauty he had met at the Horse Fair in Hertfordshire. He thought of his mother with her dark doe-like eyes and jet, black hair, very much like Naspa, the Sitka girl he had turned to after he thought he lost Penny for good. Naspa had died when their son was born.

Bitter feelings welled up in him when he remembered how he called the doctor, but when he saw the Indian girl, he said, "I don't treat squaws. Get the medicine man. Didn't you know you were a squaw man, Long."

Will felt angry then. And he was still angry at the way the gentle Indians were being treated by the white settlers. This was the reason he had brought the boy home with him. Naspa's sisters would have raised him within the tribe, but Will had been afraid he'd grow up to be an underdog, lacky to the whites.

Now he had the problem of explaining all this to Penny. Was it asking too much to expect her to understand?

He saw her immediately, sitting in the bay window of the Mermaid. She had dressed, with, great care, which only served to make Will very conscious of his corduroys and plain shirt. He wore a coloured kerchief around his neck; Penny was reminded of the gypsy men who worked in the fields when she was a child. She kept these thoughts to herself.

Will asked what she would like to drink. Poor fellow, he was almost tongue-tied.

"Shall we just have lemonade?" she suggested, smiling. "It is so nice; we could take a picnic down to the river."

"That's a good idea. I could do with some nice fresh air."

Like a pair of schoolchildren, they chose cakes and rolls at the bakers. After adding two small bottles of ginger beer to their store, they made their way to the river.

Will carried Penny's cloth bag, now filled with cakes, rolls, a small brolly, and waterproof.

"Is the brolly large enough for both of us?" Penny asked, laughing.

"Only if we sit very close together."

They slipped so easily into the pattern of easy banter; was it possible to pick up the threads again? It was all so long ago. Will had changed. Perhaps his restlessness and the urge to travel were satisfied now. There was a lot she did not know about him, but she would enjoy today.

They set off over London Bridge to the city, walking as far as Smithfield, where they watched the bummarees, at work hauling the large carcasses of beef. They visited St. Paul's Cathedral and climbed the great dome. They gazed at the great sprawl of London and then went on to the tower, where they viewed the Crown Jewels.

"What a fortune they must be worth."

"More than your gold strike?"

Will laughed and said, "Much more."

Now they were hungry and made their way to the water's edge. He chose a seat near the entrance for the boats landing at the tower.

"This spot must have been the last view of the outside world for the prisoners who were sent to the tower," Will said. "Next stop, chopping block."

"Oh, Will, shut up please. I won't be able to eat my lunch if you discuss such gory details."

"That's the general idea. I shall have your share too; I am famished."

Penny laughed and spread the waterproof on the grass for them to sit on.

"Pity it isn't going to rain," he added. "Won't get the chance to get close under the brolly, after all."

After he polished off his share of the rolls and cakes, he sat back and rolled a cigarette. Penny relaxed and watched the shipping on the river.

"I think there is a lot I have to tell you," Will began; he struggled to find a way to tell Penny about his son.

"When I left Dawson City," he continued, "you had written that you were going home, but you didn't give me the address. I hoped my letters would be forwarded to you. But you never wrote again."

"I am so terribly sorry. I didn't realise I hadn't given you my address; I thought you must have forgotten me."

"I didn't forget you, but after two years, I decided I must make the best of things. After all, life had to go on. While out in Indian territory, I broke my leg badly in a fall. A band of Sitka Indians found me, and a young Indian girl nursed me. After I got better, I stayed on as a trapper. She and I were very happy together, but during the birth of our son, she died."

"Oh, Will, how awful for you."

"The doctor wouldn't help because she was an Indian." He lapsed into silence, the pain of that awful memory showing in his face.

"Where is your little boy now?" Penny asked gently.

"He is with Sally; she has been bringing Tim up with her own children. I have been helping to support the household because her husband, Andrew, is a sick man. He has a weak chest and can't hold a job down for long."

"My sister Jane had the same problem, but her husband, Jason Tebbit, sent her to a sanatorium in Switzerland. She seems much better, but she still looks very pale."

"It is a terrible condition. I worry the children may take ill with it," Will said, looking thoughtful.

Watching him, Penny wished she had the courage to tell him what happened to her. But now was not the time. If they ever became close, she must tell him of John Cooper and the anguish she had caused her family. She was curious to know more about the little boy.

"When can I meet your boy?" she asked. "And does he take after you?"

"He has dark eyes and a darker complexion than I have, so I suppose he takes after his mother." Then he added, as an afterthought, "Or perhaps he will look like a true Romany, like my mother."

"Really?" Penny's voice sounded excited. "How we used to envy the gypsy children their piebald ponies when I was a child."

Will was delighted; she had not despised him for his origins, and neither had she condemned him out of hand when he told her about Naspa, and the child. But later, when he went over their conversation in his mind, he realised she had said very, little about her own life in all that time. Could she be hiding something from him, and would he be able to live with it if he knew? Perhaps it would be best to leave well enough alone. She would tell him in her own time, anyway.

He hoped they could be good friends. It seemed unlikely they could recapture the love they had once had for each other. And for all he knew, she may have a man friend already. Had Naspa lived, he would probably have stayed in Alaska. He had been happy there. He remembered Penny as a fond memory of his youth and had been in tune with his new life. He was surprised that Penny was not married in all the time he been away. He still had not got over the surprise of seeing her again. What a coincidence.

Will whistled happily to himself as he bedded down the horse. He had asked her to go out with him again, and she had said, "I'd love to, Will."

For the moment, he was feeling happier than he had been in many months.

Sally notice Will's good spirits.

"Why did she have to turn up again and ruin our arrangement ?" she asked Andrew.

"Well, he is a young man; he's bound to want female company. He may not marry, though. How do you know if she's willing to take on the boy? I can't see him being willing to give him up, can you?"

"That's true," replied Sally. "Let's hope she doesn't want the responsibility."

But Sally was still worried. The money Will gave her made life a little easier. She no longer had to go out charring to make ends meet. And the children had filled out on the extras she had been able to buy. Nothing in the world lasts forever. They would manage somehow. But she hoped they would not have to.

As for Penny, she had very mixed feelings. She still found Will attractive, but he was different from the young man she had given her heart to all those years ago at the doctor's house. For one thing, he seemed a lot more serious. He also held firm convictions, and when he expressed an opinion, he obviously felt it was the right one, regardless of what she thought. Was he now a strong character or just pig-headed? She would doubtless find out. In the meantime, she would reserve her judgement until she knew him better.

Martha was amazed when Penny told her she had met Will again and that they had spent the afternoon together. She did not let on she had seen him coming out of the pawnbrokers a short while ago.

"Why don't you bring him to dinner one evening?" she suggested. "Stuart would love to meet him, and so would I. Is he still as handsome?"

Penny laughed and said, "I don't know about handsome. He is still very,attractive to me, but I feel I have to get to know him again."

"Do you still love him?"

Penny, look worried as she replied, "I don't know. I felt a great surge of relief when we first met again. But he is so different. Serious and at times very bitter."

"Do you know what happened to him in all those years?"

Penny recalled the bitterness and pain Will had shown when he told her about Naspa and his life as a trapper.

"Well, I know he had an accident and was nursed by an Indian girl who he lived with. They had a son. Will brought him back to England after the girl died."

"Doesn't that worry you?" Martha asked, looking quizzically at her sister.

"Not really; who am I to cast stones? I haven't been able to tell him about John."

Penny fell silent, and Martha did not pursue the subject further.

Penny waited until she was sure Will was in a good mood and then sprung it on him: "How about coming to dinner with Martha and Stuart one evening?"

"How can a rough fellow like me make small talk with a doctor?" he replied. "I am an uneducated chap with no prospects. I'm not good enough for your family; I shouldn't be seeing you. You should have married one of the farmers from your home."

Penny winced. He would never guess how close she had been to just that.

"Don't be silly, Will. It is just an invitation to a sociable meal. Martha said she'd like to see you again, and you'll like Stuart; he is such a friendly chap."

"Alright but try to make it a Saturday, in case Sally pops my best suit in hock again."

Penny laughed. "She certainly knows how to curtail your social life. Good job I don't mind seeing you in cord trousers and a kerchief around your neck."

"It's not funny," Will said with mock severity. "One day, I will dress as smart as a city gent; you'll see."

"So long as you don't smell of mothballs, I really don't mind."

Will groaned. "Don't remind me; it was awful. Must have been hanging next to someone's fur coat."

They had been to the music hall, and Will wore his suit fresh from the pawnbrokers. Even the comedian had joked about someone in the audience smelling like his Aunt Maud's closet. If only Sally would leave his blessed suit alone. He decided then he would hide it in the stable, suitably wrapped. He could not bear the thought that he would embarrass Penny in front of her relations. It was going to be hell meeting them, anyway.

Will met Penny as she came off duty. He was looking very smart. His trousers were pressed, his collar was very stiff, and he looked very self-conscious. Penny linked her arm in his, and they set off to dine with Martha and Stuart; she could smell just a hint of mothballs and carbolic soap, and his shoes had a rhythmic squeak. Penny smiled to herself. Poor Will. He was trying so, hard; if only he had more confidence. He was so nervous.

Penny rang the bell. Will shuffled his feet uncomfortably, aware that he was now committed to meeting some of Penny's family. The door opened, and there was Martha, smiling and welcoming them in. She said, "I am so pleased you were able to come, Will. Stuart is really looking forward to this evening. It isn't,often he has the chance to talk to such a travelled man as yourself. He is longing to hear about your adventures."

Will was pleased. He had not thought of himself as a travelled man.

"Hello, how nice to meet you," Stuart said, coming forward to greet them. "Sit by the fire; we can have a drink together while the girls get the meal organised."

Penny could hear their voices and gusts of laughter coming from the parlour; it was obvious the two men were getting on well.

"He still looks like the old Will to me. He hasn't lost his sense of fun." Martha went on, "Have you told him about your own life yet?"

"I don't think I can."

"You will have to, if you hope to make a new beginning with him."

Penny, busy serving the soup, replied, "I haven't made up my mind yet."

"Is it the child? Couldn't you accept him as your own?"

"I don't know. I haven't even met him yet." They relapsed into silence, concentrating on serving the meal.

"Can I give Will the breast of the bird? He won't know whether to pick the bones or not."

Martha laughed. "Do we appear so formal to him, Penny."

"He was terrified of the meeting family."

"Heaven help him when he meets Dad, then."

"Yes, he can be pretty formidable, even to us." They both laughed, remembering how cold those blue eyes could be when their father was displeased.

"I don't believe Stuart has enjoyed himself so much in a long time," Martha said, glancing affectionately at her husband, hovering over a map with Will, as they had a cup of tea.

Stuart was interested to see where exactly Will had been on the long trip to the gold fields. It had been an amazing journey. Total wilderness, mountains, blizzards. Pitted against the weather, wild animals, and at times rough characters. He himself had journeyed in Europe but was fascinated to hear of the adventures of those who went to the colonies and beyond.

"No doubt, Will, it must have been the finest adventure you will ever have."

"It was, but looking back, it seems like another life."

The meal was a great success. Later, they all helped to clear up and pack away the dishes.

Will said, "You've got yourself a grand cook, Stuart."

"Yes, and her sister's not too bad, either."

Will blushed, and they all laughed.

"I am looking for a practice outside London," Stuart announced, as they relaxed in front of the fire.

"What a shame," Penny said, surprised. "You have made this place so comfortable. Don't you like it here, Martha?"

Martha only smiled, and then Stuart said, "I have about six months to find the right one."

"Why hurry?" Will asked.

"Well, we said we wouldn't bring up a family here."

"Oh, Martha that's wonderful news." Penny, gave her sister a big hug. Stuart was smiling broadly; he was so obviously delighted.

"I have been offered a place at Iver, in Buckinghamshire. Do you know it?"

"I should say I do," Will replied. "I was brought up a stone's throw from there myself."

"We thought of going down at the weekend to look the place over. Why don't you and Penny come too? We can take a picnic. Bring your lad along. We are all keen to meet him."

Penny must have told them about the boy, but it had been mentioned so casually, as an accepted fact.

"I'm not sure I could cope with him all day; he is only three."

"Let the girls cope with him, then. Got to get their hand in sometime."

"That's a good idea," Martha butted in. She was keen to see how Penny would take to the child.

Will reluctantly, agreed he had been putting off this moment for so long. It would have to be faced, and perhaps it would be easier in company than if Penny had to meet the boy at his sister's home. Sally was so against him resuming his relationship with Penny, and he was still greatly attracted to her. It had been a passionate affair in their youth. He had loved Naspa but never with the intensity he had felt for Penny. He feared Penny might not feel the same for him again. Or that she would be unable to accept the child. Maybe Sally was right. Perhaps to pursue this desire to know her well would end in tears. But he had to find out, even if it was painful.

"How shall we go then?" Will asked Stuart.

"By train from Paddington to Bond Street Station and then Uxbridge; perhaps hire a landau for the day. That would give us the mobility to be able to have a good look around the area."

He thought for a moment and then replied, "That could be very, expensive. I'll get in touch with my dad and see if he can borrow a good size trap for us for the day."

"Shall we leave that to you then? It would be a great help to know we had transport laid on at the other end," Stuart replied.

Sally was in a very truculent mood.

"What's the rush to have the boy ready, then?" she asked belligerently.

"I told you, I am taking him to see Mum and Dad today."

"So why do you have to catch that train? You could go on any train. She is going with you, isn't she?"

"Yes, as a matter of fact she is. Any objections?"

"Well, you can see to the boy yourself." Sally flounced off.

She knew he was making a fool of himself, and she certainly was not going to help him.

Will struggled to dress his son.

"Tim, my boy, keep still a moment. You are going to see a lady, today; I want you to be a good boy." He desperately wanted today to go well. Perhaps they could stay overnight at his parents' place. Dad would not mind, but he was not sure how his mother would feel about it. He hastily packed a bag for the boy, pyjamas,and some clean changes. Finally, he popped in a clean shirt, socks, night things, and razor for himself. He glanced around the room in case there was anything else he should have taken. Then sweeping the little lad up in his arms and grabbing the bag, he left the house determined not to miss the train.

They had agreed to meet under the clock. Penny, who had arrived first, saw Will carrying a bag and holding a small boy by the hand. She felt a rush of pity for the child, who although clean had a somewhat unkempt appearance. Clothes were so obviously hand-me-downs. Breaches were too wide, the coat too short, and his dark hair stood up at the back where he had slept on it.

"Hello, Will," she said brightly. "Are you going to introduce me?"

She smiled down at the small boy and asked, "What's your name, then?"

"Tim," he replied. "What's yours?"

Will look puzzled and asked, "What can he call you, Penny?"

"Just Penny, I suppose," she replied.

"Doesn't sound very respectful, though, does it?"

Just at that moment, Martha and Stuart arrived, hot and bothered. They had a large picnic hamper, which they were carrying between them. In addition, Stuart had a large overnight bag.

"Phew. I thought we wouldn't make it in time," he said. "It took a while packing the food in this hamper. Got to look after the inner man and boy, haven't we?"

Stuart bent down and gently lifted the little lad up. "Come and see the hot train we will be travelling on," he said to Tim.

"Hot train?" Tim echoed; he liked the sound of it, so he said it again: "Hot train, hot train."

He sat on the seat, watching them stow the bags in the luggage rack, his big eyes taking in everything around him.

Soon, there was a banging of doors and heavy breathing of the engine as it got up to steam, and then a whistle. They were off.

Tim looked out of the window for a while, chattering at all he saw. When his interest waned, Martha opened the picnic basket and took out a small bar of chocolate. Inwardly, Will groaned. Tim would get in an awful mess, and he had not thought to bring a wet flannel or a towel to clean him up. Sure enough, Tim soon had a large ring of chocolate around his face and all over his fingers.

"Here, let me clean you up a bit." Will took his handkerchief from his pocket.

"Don't worry," Penny said as she took a sponge and small towel from her bag. "Here we are, Tim; shall we wash your hands and face?"

He reluctantly allowed her to gently wipe his hands, but he protested when she tried to remove the ring from his face.

"Do you want to see something funny?" she asked.

Tim nodded, and then Penny held him up to look in the mirror above the seat. He began to chuckle. Then she handed him the flannel and helped him clean his face. Soon, he was engrossed in a cloth book that Stuart had given him. Penny explained the pictures to him. Will glanced at Martha; she smiled at him, and he felt he was among friends, accepted as one of them. Looking at his little boy, so obviously happy as he was, Will knew that what he most wanted was a home, a warm home, with Penny waiting for him, with Tim happy and well cared for. He was aware of the shabby clothes and pinched cheeks of his son. Sally didn't really want the responsibility of the boy. She had enough to do looking after her own children and sick husband. When at last the train pulled into Vine Street Station, Jim Logan, a friend of Will's father, was waiting for them with a large trap.

He was a pleasant man, with a slight brogue of his native Scotland; he had worked with Will's father at the rubber works for many years. As they sped along the country lanes, he became quite talkative.

"Will's dad is alright," he told Penny. "He just has a terrible thirst. It's working with the hot rubber all day that does it. Now his mum's different again. If she takes to you, she'll be a friend for life, but if she doesn't, you'll have a thorn in your side forever. She is a gypsy, you know, a good-looking woman in her youth."

"Give over, Jim," Will said, laughing. "She doesn't want to hear all the family faults."

"Alright, but before I forget, your mother says you are to bring Miss Thompson to stay overnight, and she has a bed made for young Timmy too."

Will was relieved; his mother could have taken the same attitude as Sally, then he would not have known what to do about the boy.

As the day wore on, little Tim became tired and grew fretful. They had had a wonderful time, picnicking by the river, looking at houses to see where Martha and Stuart would like to live, and generally taking in the country scene and fresh air. It had been warm and bright, and the blossoms were a picture in the thatched cottage gardens.

Along the banks, the early spring flowers were out in profusion, and they heard the gentle hum of bees.

"I think we should book you into the local inn and take Timmy to see his grandparents now." Penny was trying to comfort the hot and dishevelled little boy.

"I think you are right," Stuart replied. "Tim looks all in, and we shall need to get washed and tidied up before going to see Dr Millard. He has invited us to dinner with him and his wife. I have met him but not his wife. For Martha, it will be the first meeting with the people I'm going to be working with."

"Well, good luck," Penny quipped. "Don't slurp your soup, Martha."

"Well, of all the nerve." Martha directed a quick kick at Penny's shins.

"Now then, do you want a referee?" Will exclaimed amid the laughter. "You'll do nothing for Martha's self-confidence saying things like that." Then he added, "Just as well we're not coming with you. You should hear Penny eating celery."

The next kick was directed at him.

The trap swung into the courtyard of the inn. Jim helped Martha down and carried their bags inside.

"He's a nice chap, knows the landlord too, so you should get a comfortable room."

Stuart was very, grateful. "Thanks, Will; it was great to have transport and not have to worry about getting a bed for the night; shall we see you tomorrow?"

"Of course; we'll pick you up after lunch, about two, then we can catch the four o'clock train back to town."

"That sounds fine; shall I pay Jim Logan today?"

"No, I will see to that," Will replied, "and thanks for a lovely day."

Jim came out of the inn and said, "I have fixed up a good room for you; they will serve Sunday dinner if you want it."

"Thank you very much, Jim," Martha said. "You're a real treasure."

He gave a little bow and smiled. "All part of the service."

"I said we'd pick them up tomorrow at about two o 'clock. Is that okay, Jim?"

"Yes, that's fine. Cheerio for now, then," he replied, pulling on the reins to turn the trap.

"Goodbye and good luck," Penny called out.

"And you too, Penny," Martha replied.

"Come on, then, old boy; gee up." Jim turned the horse towards Will's parents' home. "He'll be glad to see his stable tonight. It's been a long day for him."

"It was very, good of you, Jim, to help us out like this. Let me know what I owe you for today and tomorrow, and I will settle up."

"No, lad, it's been my pleasure to help you out."

"Please let me pay for some oats and hay for the horse." Will did not want to take advantage of his parents' friendship with Jim.

As if sensing this, Jim replied, "Alright, if you insist. Dobbin won't say no to hay and oats."

Jim dropped them off outside the gate. "I won't come in now; tell Thomas I will drop in to see him and Eliza later in the week."

"Okay, Jim; see you tomorrow then."

Tim had fallen asleep on Penny's shoulder. "Poor little fellow," she said. "He's had enough for one day."

Eliza, Will's mother, had heard the trap pull up at the door. "Come on in," she called. Then seeing the sleeping child, she whispered to Penny, "Bring him in here," leading the way to a small room where the child's bed was made up.

Penny laid him gently on the coverlet and carefully removed his shoes. Will's mother covered him with a warm blanket and then tiptoed out of the room.

"It would be a shame to wake him now," she said.

Although Will's mother was a haughty-looking woman, Penny felt the warmth of a smile which extended to her eyes as she spoke to her. She at once felt, here was a friend. They returned to the kitchen, where the men were sitting and talking.

"I expect you're ready for a cup of tea?" Eliza asked.

"Yes, please, Mrs Long," Penny said, smiling.

"Penny," she said, "you're not a bit like I expected."

Penny felt confused; was she disappointed?

Eliza continued, "The way you handle the boy was as if you were used to children."

Will spoke up. "Well, she is a nurse, Mum, and you've worked on the children's ward, haven't you, Penny?"

"Well, Will, that boy needs more attention than Sally is able to give him."

Will sighed and said, "I know, Mum, but I'm not going to let you take on my responsibilities. It is not fair. You, raised seven of us. You've done your share."

The subject was dropped. Penny wondered if she could cope with the idea of a ready-made family, if her relationship with Will became more serious? What if they had children of their own? Would she be able to feel the same about Tim then? There was time to think of that if they decided they had a future together.

Later that evening, Penny helped Will's mother clear up the supper dishes, while the two men had a quiet chat and a pipe of tobacco together.

"I was so pleased to have Will home again," Eliza said. "It's a big worry when your boys take off on the Gold Rush. We still don't know what became of Tom. I lay awake thinking of him. He was our first-born, and as much as we love the others, he always had a special place in our heart."

Penny did not know what to say. She gently put her arm around the older woman's shoulder and said, "It will all come right someday, I'm sure."

Eliza wiped a tear from her eye, squared her shoulders, and replied, "This won't do. I can't, afford the luxury of feeling sorry for myself. Come on; I'll show you the garden."

It had been a long time since Penny had seen such a profusion of flowers and vegetables. The scent of cloves from the pinks lining the path gave the warm evening a heady fragrance.

Presently, the others came out to join them. It was one of those rare evenings, warm and still, when every scent and sound is crystal clear.

Eventually, the dusk almost upon them, and the mosquitoes beginning to trouble them, they moved back indoors.

Tim woke, and after a spot of supper, he was washed and changed, but it wasn't long before he became sleepy again and settled down for the night. Penny had been in to tuck him up. Looking down at the small child sleeping there, she knew that if she was to marry Will, she'd have to love this little boy. How could you not grow to love him, with his pale cheeks and big, solemn eyes? Penny was sure that Will wanted to ask her to marry him, but guessed he was worried if she would take to the child. Seeing him lying there, she had an overwhelming desire to give him a hug. He needed love.

The following morning, Penny awoke to the sound of crowing, clucking, and quacking. It was feeding time for the poultry and pigs that Will's father kept at the bottom of their long garden. A brass jug of hot water had been placed on the marble-topped washstand. She washed and dressed quickly. The smell of bacon drifted up the stairs.

Penny peaked into Tim's room; his bed was empty. She hurried downstairs.

"I am sorry," she said on entering the kitchen. "I seem to be the last down for breakfast."

"Good morning, Penny," Eliza said warmly. "You looked so comfortable, we let you sleep in; come and have your breakfast now. Will, pour Penny a cup of tea."

"Pour me one at the same time," Will's dad said, pushing his cup towards his son. "What are your plans for today? Young Tim is busy feeding the ducks."

"Well, we are picking up Martha and Stuart from the inn at about two o'clock. I thought we would spend the last few hours with you both," Will replied.

It was surprising how quickly the time went. Penny helped Will's mother prepare the Sunday dinner, while Will and his dad kept an eye on young Tim and the poultry. They certainly had more grain than usual, as Tim filled his little bucket several times and scattered it liberally.

Puffing away at their pipes, the two men chatted, every now and then roaring with laughter.

"Get those two together," Eliza said, "and you hear some pretty tall tales."

"Just hearing Will laugh is infectious," Penny replied. "But he doesn't laugh as much as he used to."

"Well, it's been a difficult time for him during the last few years. It's left a mark on him, as I expect it has on you too. Don't let your happiness escape you now. True love is fragile. Not everyone is lucky enough to find it."

Just at that moment, the men came into the kitchen.

"How about a nice cup of tea, then?" Thomas said. "All this jawing is thirsty work. Mind you, having a cup of tea was my downfall you know, Penny."

"Really? How was that?"

"Well, I went to a horse fair up at Hemel Hempstead. It was a hot day; after I had struck a bargain for a horse, the fellow said, 'Let's go for a drink.' Now I never refuse refreshment, so I went with him. Well, he was a travelling man, and he led me to his caravan. There on the steps of the van was this beautiful girl, Eliza, who made me a cup of tea. Later, I walked with her in the moonlight. I was in love."

"How did you manage to keep in touch when the horse fair was over?"

"I followed the vans. Where they went, I went, doing casual work wherever I could. An older traveller whose wife died let me move in with him; his wife had been a *gadzo*, a nongypsy, like me. He taught me to make pegs and baskets, and to shoe horses, sharpen knives, and repair saucepans and buckets. I learnt herbal cures; he was teaching me the Romany language too. We travelled all over to the horse fairs. I learnt to break his horses for him, for he was getting old and had no sons of his own.

"After two years, I was tolerated but not totally accepted by the family. Whenever I mentioned marriage to Eliza's father, he refused. Whenever they tried to arrange a marriage for her, she refused. Eventually, we eloped and then returned to ask their forgiveness, but they never really forgave me because gadzo are considered impure by the Romanies. We continued to live with the old man.

"Eventually, we arrived in Scotland to pick the raspberries. That's when things really went wrong for us. The old man died. Eliza was pregnant with our first child. After a trip to town, we returned to the campsite, only to find the caravan burning. It was the custom when the last of the family had died to burn the caravan with all the linen. The livestock, plates, and valuables had been shared out among his extended family. Probably a custom left over from when the tribes left India, and they would have a funeral pyre. Whatever the reason, it left us with no home. Eliza's father said she could return to live with them, but he was adamant there was no place for me.

"I was at my wit's end about what to do. Eliza's mother couldn't be seen to go against her man. But she came and spoke with me. She promised to take care of Eliza and the baby, and said she trusted me to make some provision for them. I can tell you, I was heartbroken when we parted."

"It must have been hard for you both; whatever did you do?"

"Well, I had to get shelter for the night, and indeed, that night, I met a crofter who took me home with him. His name was Jim Logan, the same Jim Logan who took you round in his horse and trap this weekend.

He lived with his mother, who was a wonderful woman; when she heard about our predicament, she took us both in and cared for Eliza until the baby came. I could never repay her for her kindness. We stayed for two months after the baby was born. Then my father wrote to say there was a job going at the rubber works, with a small company cottage to go with it. So I took it and in fact stayed with the firm and eventually worked my way up to manager. It was hard for Liza; she seldom saw her mother, but we have been happy and raised a fine family."

All this time, Eliza had been quiet; turning to Penny, she said, "It was hard, but I would do it again if I had my time over again."

Will puffed on his pipe thoughtfully and then said, "You know, I think the way you both worked to bring up the family and the sacrifices you made for each other, both of you deserve a medal."

At this, Eliza laughed and said, "Less of the flannel, young Will. Let's get the dinner dished up. Fetch Tim in and get his hands washed while your father carves."

Busy at the stove, warming the plates and dishing the vegetables, Eliza's mind was definitely on the present. No doubt if Will's father was a bit of a dreamer, his wife was a very practical person.

Penny felt she had got to know Will's parents amazingly well in the short time she had been with them. After dinner, Jim Logan arrived to take them to pick up Martha and Stuart, and then on to the station to catch the train back to London. Penny was sorry the time sped by so quickly. She had enjoyed the day and the warm welcome she had received.

Eliza and Thomas saw them off, waving until they were out of sight. Tim was very fretful. He didn't want to return to his Aunt Sally after the attention he had enjoyed at his grandparents. They were a few minutes early arriving at the inn. While they waited for Martha and Stuart they chatted with Jim.

"I shall be giving up the haulage soon, Will. I'm not getting any younger, and I have put a bit aside for my old age. I suppose a young fellow like you wouldn't like to take it on?"

Will was completely taken by surprise and said, "But I have no money to speak of. How could I pay for the horses and equipment? Never mind the yard and stables. Also, I'd have to find a cottage or somewhere to live."

"Well, you think it over; you don't have to find it all at once. You could buy me out over a two-year period."

"I'll think about it over this week. I'll come again next week and let you know what I decide to do."

Will's mind was in a turmoil. He certainly hadn't expected this.

"Okay; there is no hurry. I have the chance for a cottage myself, so if you do decide to have the business, you could have the house as well." Jim got down to take the bags from Martha and Stuart, who had now emerged from the inn.

During the journey back to London, he had no chance to talk with Penny. Martha and Stuart were very excited about his new job and the prospect of a new home.

Martha had got on well with both Dr Millard and his wife.

"They have a lovely, thatched house with stables and paddocks for the horses. It will be a proper partnership," she told them. "Stuart will have his own patients, and each doctor will stand in for the other for holidays and days off. And another thing: they have a young family themselves. I think we will get on well with them."

"Another bit of luck is that we have seen a house that could suit us," Stuart said, looking a little anxious. " It needs a bit doing to it, and I must arrange a loan to buy it. But it's less than half a mile from the Millards and has four bedrooms and an outbuilding to have a trap and horse."

"It certainly sounds like everything is going to fall into place for you both." Penny was genuinely pleased for her sister.

"Well, I hope you're right, Penny." Stuart sighed. "It's so difficult to tie up the ends; I should get myself a good solicitor tomorrow."

Will sat quietly, thinking, *If only everything would turn out well for us too*. Penny was playing with young Tim. They looked so happy together; surely it could work out. He could only hope.

"You are very quiet, Will," Penny said, smiling. "Penny for your thoughts."

"Now that is a pun, if you like," quipped Stuart. And they all laughed.

"I have a lot on my mind," Will said. "Jim Logan wants to retire and has offered me his business. I have been doing carrier work out of Borough Market. There is more traffic in London but more competition too. He has regular contracts with local millers and farmers, and he is offering the house and buildings on loan, something I could never afford in London."

"Why don't you jump at the chance and have a go?" Stuart suggested.

"It needs a lot of careful thought. I don't know if it would generate enough business to pay the mortgage and run a home."

"Well, if you married Penny, you wouldn't have to have a housekeeper," Stuart said, glancing sideways at Penny, whose blush matched the roots of her hair.

Will squirmed with embarrassment and said lamely, "Err, I couldn't expect Penny to accept that kind of insecurity. I would have to make a go of it first, wouldn't I?"

"Do I have any say in this?" Penny cried out, indignant.

"Well, would you marry him if he asked you?"

"I'm not answering that, Stuart. Will hasn't asked me, and I'll thank you not to try to create a marriage mart on my account."

Martha tactfully changed the subject and gave Stuart a look which clearly said, "Don't you dare make any more remarks like that."

When they finally disembarked at Paddington, Will asked Penny if he could see her during the week, but she said, "No, I'm sorry, Will, but I have to help out at the London Hospital at Whitechapel. They are terribly short of nurses because of an outbreak of hepatitis."

"When will you be off duty again?"

"Not until Saturday morning," she replied.

"Will you meet me here then and come down to see Jim Logan with me? I have to give him my decision, and we haven't had a chance to talk."

Penny knew she would need to rest after the week she had ahead, but his eyes pleaded with her to say yes.

"Alright, but could we make it midday to give me a few hours' rest?"

"That's fine, then." Will leaned over and gave Penny a kiss. "It's going to seem a long week without seeing you."

Martha glared at Stuart; she wanted him to keep quiet and not make any more wisecracks, but he just winked at her.

"Well, it was a lovely weekend," Will said as he helped Tim into his coat. "Thanks for suggesting it, Stuart."

Stuart smiled down at Tim and asked, "Did you enjoy yourself, young fella?"

"Yes," was the reply. "Hot train! Hot train."

"Good lad." He couldn't help laughing. "Tim is mad about the trains, anyway."

Martha and Stuart said goodbye to Will and Tim, and,took a cab back to their house; Penny had spent the night there before going on to Whitechapel on Monday morning.

Martha was very excited as she asked her sister, "Do you think Will is going to ask you to marry him, Penny? Wouldn't it be wonderful if you were living close to us?"

Penny smiled and said, "Not so fast, Martha; he hasn't asked me yet. And have you thought what Mum and Dad would say if they knew he was part gypsy with an illegitimate son?"

"Surely it's what you feel about him that matters," Stuart said, looking thoughtful. "It isn't anyone's right to make that decision for you."

"And you do love him, don't you, Penny?" Martha asked earnestly.

Penny laughed and said, "You are an incurable romantic, Martha. I am thinking about it, though."

CHAPTER 11

A Time for Decisions

ß & ß

Penny didn't have a lot of time during the following week to ponder her own problems. She was rushed off her feet all week. The hospital was crowded with so many sick people. The shortage of staff was so acute that she found herself doing all sorts of tasks just to keep the ward and patients sanitary.

The area was beset by extreme poverty. Clean water had always been a problem. Many inhabitants shared one water cock, using the water over and over again, until they threw it back into the street, homes having neither sinks nor cesspools. Penny knew that Joseph Bazalgette, had overseen the laying of the sewers, but few slum properties were connected. No one had money to pay the fee.

Consequently, diarrhoea was a killer of children, in particular.

Tending small, dehydrated children, Penny was filled with compassion. If Will did ask her to marry him, she was determined she would take young Tim into her heart and give him the chance to grow up strong in good country air.

On the broad pavement on the northern side of Whitechapel Road was the most amazing street market. Food such as jellied eels, hot pies, and fruit; quack medicines; and toys and flowers were on sale side by side with acrobats, musicians, and strong men performing for the crowds. Fierce competition between the Jewish and Irish stallholders with their second- hand clothes and shouts of the costermongers all added to the cosmopolitan atmosphere. She had never experienced anything like it before. By the light of greasy oil burners and candles, the trading went on until midnight. It was an impressive sight, in spite, of the poverty. It was something Penny would never forget.

Will was struck by how pale Penny looked when she met him at the station.

"Have you been waiting long?" she asked him.

"No, not too long," he said. "Are you alright? You look very tired."

She smiled. "I will be alright when I've had some fresh air; it has been a very,hard week. I wouldn't want to work there all the time. I don't know how they cope with it, day in and day out. Those poor people. The conditions over there are awful. No wonder so many people, especially children, get ill."

"I know, it's pretty grim," he said. "The overcrowding makes it worse."

Seeing the concern on his face, Penny asked, "Anyway, how was your week? And where is Tim?"

"Well, I have had a lot of thinking to do this week, and as I wanted to talk to you, just us two, I left Tim with Sally. She thinks I am giving Jim Logan a hand this weekend."

Penny nodded; she didn't like this, subterfuge, but knowing how Sally had taken exception to their friendship, it didn't surprise her.

"Shall we have a cup of tea or get on the train first?" she asked.

"Let's get on the train and have a cup of tea when we reach Uxbridge."

"Okay," Penny said, opening her bag to get her purse. "Let's get our tickets and see if we can find a compartment to ourselves."

"No, I will buy them," he objected. "After all, I asked you to come."

"No, Will. I insist on paying my share; it's not as if I have any responsibilities. All my salary is my own."

Will felt some misgivings when he heard this, after agreeing to let her pay her share. Would she be willing to give up her independence for him? Was he expecting too much?

Tickets, purchased, they made their way along the train until they found an empty compartment.

"This one will do." Penny opened the door and scrambled up the awkward step. "The trouble with travelling by train is the door; it ruins the hems." She tried to brush off the soot with her hanky.

"You're funny," Will said, laughing. "You've made it worse; the soot is all greasy."

"I knew I shouldn't wear my best, but I wanted to look nice to see your family."

"Don't worry; you look lovely to me."

"Oh, Will, you, flatterer." And with that, she leaned over and surprised him with a kiss.

He put his arms around her and gave her a big hug. "Marry me, Penny," he said. "Please marry me. I can't offer you much, only love and hard work, but I don't want to ever lose you again."

"I couldn't bear to part with you again either, Will. I've never stopped loving you. But after all that happened, it's a miracle that we have a second chance. I often cursed myself for letting you go."

"I can't offer you security, but if we wait for that, life may pass us by. Will you take a chance, darling?"

Penny decided never to repeat the mistake she made before; this time, she wouldn't ask for security, only love.

"Yes, I will take a chance," she replied.

"And what about Tim?" Will asked hesitantly. "Do you think you could love him too?"

"I will do my best to be a good mother to him. He is a lovely little boy. I feel sure if I am kind to him, he will respond, and we shall grow to love one another."

He put his arm around Penny and gave her a kiss. "I am so pleased you feel that way. I hoped you would. It's a lot to ask, but you really are a remarkable woman. When I first met you, you were a maid, then you became a housekeeper, and now nurse, and the climax of your career is yet to come: wife of William Long, carrier extraordinaire."

Penny laughed and said, "Well, life has certainly taken some extraordinary twists and turns. But the climax will surely be when we tell my mum and dad."

Will turned glum; he hadn't met Mr and Mrs Thompson yet. But he knew from what Penny told him about her childhood that they were staunch chapel people. He wondered how they would feel about his gypsy blood, never mind the fact that he had an illegitimate child, also of a different race. He knew they supported missionaries to foreign lands; would they consider this match too close to home?

"Cheer up," Penny said, noticing his fallen countenance. "It's not the end of the world. I've said yes, haven't I? Once they've met you, they will welcome you into the family."

"I only hope you're right."

They sat in silence for a while, busy with their own thoughts.

Will was the first to speak: "We must get Jim Logan to show us the house, then we must find out if the business will see us alright. Having to borrow the money to get started worries me because there may not be enough coming in to keep us and pay off the mortgage."

"That could be a problem," Penny replied. "But if it has enough rooms, we could take in lodgers."

"I don't like the idea, but I suppose it would help in an emergency."

By now, they were both excitedly making plans. Will thought to himself what a good thing Penny had broken the ice by giving him that unexpected kiss.

"Penny," he said suddenly. "Had you planned to give me a kiss like that?"

"Yes," she replied cheekily. "If I hadn't, you would have been too tongue-tied to ask me."

"I was afraid you would say no."

"And I was afraid you'd never ask," she retorted.

Laughing, they disembarked at Uxbridge. Jim Logan, waiting with the trap, saw that happiness on their faces as they came towards him.

"Hello, you two; you're looking mighty pleased with yourselves."

"We are going to be married, Jim, and you're the first to know."

"That's wonderful news," he said, beaming at Penny. "He needs a good woman to keep him in order."

"Now then, Jim, that's enough of that. I don't want you to make her change her mind."

Still smiling, Jim flicked the reins, and they moved off.

"What did you want to see first," Jim asked: "the house or the business?"

"We'd like to see the house first," Will answered, "and then I'd like Dad to go over the business things with us. I could do with his advice."

Then turning to Penny, Will said, "I thought if we had a look at the house together, you could decide if you like it. Then if Dad gives me the benefit of his experience with the business details, we could discuss it tonight and decide if we think it's a good proposition for us."

"That is a good idea," Penny said, "because I haven't any business experience, and your dad will be pleased if you ask his advice."

"What do you think, Jim?" Will asked.

He looked thoughtful and then said, "I am the seller, but if you don't think it's right for you, don't be afraid to say no. I think it would give you a start. But I am not a family man. I stayed with my mother after Dad died. Somehow, I never got around to marriage. Tom and Liza will be able to help you decide. But you are under no obligation and no hard feelings if you decide not to take it."

"Thanks, Jim; you are a real friend."

"I hope so. Liza and Thomas were good to me when Mother died. I stayed with them at first, and he got me a job in the rubber factory. It gave me a start until I was on my feet, so I'd like to do the same for them now, by helping you."

After a short ride, they arrived at the house. It was old and dirty, white with black beams and a thatched roof that had seen better days. Inside, it was shabby in a way that showed it lacked a woman's touch. In her mind, Penny could visualise it with bright paint, new curtains, and polished floors.

Will was more concerned with what needed repairing and if the roof leaked.

"I think I could thatch the roof myself," he said, "but I don't know whether I could repair the woodwork on the sills and fix the doors."

Jim looked amused and replied, "Well, we will take the dilapidation into account in the price. Come and see the stables and outhouses now."

He led them across the yard to the stable. Here it was a different story altogether. The building was in a good state of repair, and the tack was all carefully hung and cleaned. The food store was well stocked, and the wagon and traps were stored in a dry area. Two mares were in the stalls, tucking into hay and oats. Both had a wonderful gloss to their coats. It was obvious their master cared more for their comfort than his own.

"There is everything you need to get started here: ladders, ropes, forks, picks, saws, small hand tools, and a bench." Jim was obviously proud of this collection.

"What are those white things there in the corner?" Penny asked.

"Those are the lifts for the beehives."

"Beehives as well?"

"Yes, and hens, ducks, and geese."

"I don't like geese," Penny said.

"Don't let the old gander hear you say, that," Jim said, laughing, "or he'll be after you. Never let him know you are afraid because it's mainly bravado on his part."

They came out of the outhouses and walked around a small orchard, where half a dozen very old hens were, dust-bathing.

"The hens are rather old ladies," Jim explained, "but they'll make good broody hens; you can raise a few more goslings for Christmas. The ducks are away on the stream; they come home for their tea, but you need to keep them shut up until they have laid, or you'll never get their eggs. Now where are those geese?" He glanced around. "Oh, no; they are in the kitchen garden again." Swearing under his breath, he picked up a stick and set off in a hurry.

Will looked at Penny; she was obviously enjoying herself.

"What do you think of it so far?" he asked.

"I think it's amazing; a few hours ago, I didn't even know if you would ask me to marry you. Now we are viewing our own kitchen garden."

"Well," he replied, "mustn't let the grass grow under my feet."

Before she could think of her reply to that, Jim came around the corner with a goose under each arm.

"Turn them into the shed," he called out after releasing them and turning back again. "I shall have to fix the fence, or there will be no vegetables left."

They were heading straight for Penny; she felt somewhat daunted by their size and the hissing gander. He was white with the palest light blue eyes. Penny stood her ground, and at the last minute, he swerved and headed into the shed.

"That's the way," Jim said. "Never let him get away with his nonsense." He barricaded the shed door. "I'll see to them later. Let's have a cup of tea now."

Penny was glad to sit for a while and recover. Her confrontation with the gander had really frightened her. How much worse would he be when his mate had goslings? She couldn't bear thinking about it.

Will put his cup back on the kitchen table, pulled his chair back and stood up.

"Not a bad sized kitchen, will you be leaving the dresser? It would be too large for a cottage, I imagine."

"We can talk about it if you decide on the place. I haven't sorted it all out yet."

"Well, we will go now, then we can have a talk with Mum and Dad and make up our minds. We haven't told them our news yet. Would you come over this evening? Then we can have another chat and sort out the details if we decide to go ahead."

Will tried to sound, matter-of-fact, but the excitement he was feeling showed through.

"Sure. See you later, then," Jim said, showing them to the door.

"Thank you for the cup of tea and the tour," Penny said. "It was lovely."

"You're welcome, lass," Jim replied. "It was my pleasure."

Penny and Will, holding hands and deep in conversation, set off at a brisk pace for his parents' house. They were in the garden, and Eliza saw them first.

"Just look at those two lovebirds," she said. "Looks as though things are going well. Soon have wedding bells. Do you think he has asked her yet?"

"By the look of them," Thomas replied, "I would say it's settled."

The young couple saw them in the garden and called out, "Hello."

"Hello," Eliza replied. "Have you just arrived?"

"No," Will answered. "We've been having a look around Jim Logan's place."

"What did you make of it? He is giving up, you know."

"Well, the house needs a bit doing to it," Will said. "But the horses and equipment look really good."

"Do you think you will take it on?" his father asked.

"I wanted to ask your advice about the price and see if there were any snags in the deal."

"Well, there is one I can see right away," Eliza said. "You will have a long way to go and see Penny."

"No, I won't. Because that is the best piece of news: We are to be married."

Thomas smiled and gave a knowing look at his wife. Eliza was delighted. She wondered what was to happen to Tim but decided to keep quiet about it for the moment. In the meantime, if they came to live at Jim Logan's place, she and Thomas would be able to enjoy their company. All their other youngsters had flown the nest, and there were times she wished she could see them more often. The place was so quiet without young people around.

By the time they returned to London, Penny's head was in a whirl. Not only was she going to marry Will, but they had a house and business lined up; she was unfamiliar with the area, so that will mean getting to know new people and returning to village life, which she had been away from for several years. There was also little Tim to consider. It will be very strange for him, she reflected. Not only had he always lived in a town, but he would have to get used to her too. Sally had doubtless been a mother figure to him, which was a daunting prospect. But Will's mother would be there to help, and she was very fond of the boy.

"You're very quiet, Penny," Will said, his voice pulling her back from her thoughts.

"I was just thinking, that's all."

"No second thoughts?" he asked.

"No, none at all." She looked thoughtful. "But we still must break the news to my folks and to Sally."

"I know, and I must admit I'm not looking forward to telling Sally; I just never know how she will react."

"I shall write to Mum and Dad tomorrow."

After saying goodbye to Will at the station, Penny returned to the nurses' home. Although many things were going through her mind, she was resolved to put everything on one side and get a good night's sleep. She was exhausted. The previous week at Whitechapel had been a hard one, and this weekend had hardly been restful. Life surely could not go on at this pace forever.

Next morning, she rose early and wrote a letter to her parents and told them they had met again. She explained what had happened to Will in the Klondike and told her about Tim and his mother, who had been an Indian girl. She also told them that Will's mother had been a Romany. She told them she loved Will and intended to marry him.

She dropped the letter in the post, wondering what their reaction would be to her news. She knew her parents were good Christian people and hoped they would not be disappointed in her again. She could not expect them to be overjoyed that Will was part gypsy. The gypsies had always been a people apart, viewed with suspicion wherever they went. Having a child outside of wedlock would be bound to be frowned upon. She could only hope they would be charitable and accept things the way they were.

That night, after she came off duty, she called on Martha to tell her the news. She was also anxious to see how their plans for their new home and Stuart's practice were going.

Martha was delighted to see Penny.

"Come on in," she said. "I have a lot to tell you."

"I have lots to tell you too."

They went through to the kitchen, where Martha put the kettle on.

"I don't suppose you have had your tea, have you?" she asked Penny.

"No," she replied. "I came straight over after work."

"If we have a cup of tea and a piece of cake now, can you stay for dinner when Stuart comes in?"

"Well, I could, but I'd be travelling home in the dark."

"So, don't. Stay the night. You can have a lift to the hospital with Stuart in the morning."

Penny was tempted to accept. "Do you think he would mind?"

"Not as long as you are up and ready when he is." Martha sat down and poured the tea. "Well, whose news first then?"

"Mine," Penny replied. "Otherwise, I shall burst."

"I knew it! You're going to marry Will, aren't you?"

"Yes, and,come to live near you."

"Oh, that's marvellous. It will be like it was when we were children. We'll be able to roam the fields and hedgerows with our children and see them grow up in the country." Martha was so excited.

"Yes, it will be lovely for us. But isn't it sad that Mum and Dad won't be close enough to enjoy their grandchildren?"

"I hadn't thought of that, Penny. I've been away from home for so long, I don't feel that I belong anymore. Besides, they have Jason and Jane and young Peter. He spends a lot of time helping Dad on the land, and Jane often keeps Mum company."

Penny knew this was true, but in her heart, she still felt this pang of sadness. She had been close to her mother, in particular. She knew how much she missed her mother's company and would have liked her children to have the chance to forge the loving relationship that distance would deny them. She had forgone that chance for them, when she turned down John Cooper and returned to London. It was sad, she reflected, that parents seldom see their children if they have to make their lives so far away. If only the cost wasn't so prohibitive.

"When will you and Stuart move into your house?" she asked.

"Not for two months, at least; there are some alterations to be done, and Stuart has to work at least two months' notice here."

"I wanted to ask you, are you making your own curtains?"

"I don't think so. Stuart wanted the decorators to put in new poles, and I thought I'd get one of the firms which does a making up service when you buy the materials to do it. I shall be getting near my time, so I hope to have it done for me."

Penny had been so busy thinking about her own plans that she almost forgot the reason her sister and brother-in-law had decided to move the country was the baby.

"Of course. How silly of me. Could I borrow your sewing machine to make ours? I shan't have a lot to spare; neither of us has much saved, and we can't be sure what we'll have coming in. I shall get the material off the market." Penny didn't want to give the impression that she was poor, only that she was trying to be prudent.

"You can borrow the sewing machine, but not for a week or two, because I am making baby clothes." Martha spoke hesitantly; she had a reputation in the family for not being much of a needlewoman. In fact, her father had been known to say, "Give Martha a John Bull puncture outfit, and she'd stick a patch on anything." This wasn't quite fair, but she wasn't the type to spend countless hours on mending and sewing. So Penny was surprised to hear that she would attempt her baby layette.

"Can I see what you've been doing so far?" she asked.

"Only if you promise not to find fault," Martha replied.

She went to fetch her sewing. Penny was aware of how much her father's sarcastic jokes had wounded Martha's self-esteem. Criticism, she decided, was very demoralising. Just because a child's first attempts were not very promising, they should not be criticised. This she now realised was what had made them so afraid of their father. He had not understood that encouragement was what they needed.

"Here we are then." Martha laid the box on the table and began to take out the most exquisite little clothes. Carefully wrapped in tissue paper were a beautiful christening robe, smocked dresses, petticoats, and bonnets.

"Why, they are so beautiful," Penny exclaimed.

"Do you really think so?" Martha's face was flushed with pleasure. "I was worried I wouldn't be able to make much of a job of it. At home, someone was always watching to see if I went wrong, and Mother was always so good at dressmaking. I felt inadequate."

"What a shame! It just goes to show what you can do, when, you set your mind to it." Penny helped to refold the little clothes, replacing them in the tissue. "When I have children, I hope I can give them self-confidence as well as love."

Penny packed the last of the little clothes in the box. "But then," she mused, "they might grow up to be terribly unruly."

Martha laughed. "I expect we shall make our own mistakes. After all. everyone is a learner when it comes to bringing up children."

Martha took the box of clothes to put away. Penny, left to herself, went to the kitchen and started to prepare vegetables for the evening meal. She was happy to think that when she started her new life with Will, she would have her sister so close by.

They shared so many interests and would be able to help one another with the children. Next year, Tim would start school; this meant she had just one year to build a loving relationship with him before a wealth of other people came into his small world. Having Martha and Stuart on hand for emergencies and moral support gave her confidence for the struggle ahead. Because in her heart of hearts, she felt it would be a struggle. Penny was too practical a girl to believe that love really conquered all.

When Martha returned, they prepared the rest of the meal together; presently, Stuart came in.

"To what do we owe this unexpected visit?" he asked after greeting them both.

"Will and I are to be married." Penny smiled at her brother-in-law. "And we shall be coming to live near you. Will is buying Jim Logan's business."

"That is wonderful news," he replied. "You should have brought him over with you. We ought to crack a bottle to celebrate."

After they had eaten, Martha, Stuart, and Penny sat and talked of their many plans, for the future. Both couples were going to be short of money to start. Part of Stuart's earnings would go towards paying towards his share of the practice, Dr Millard having put up the money to buy out the retiring doctor. But it was unlikely that they would not do well. While for Penny and Will, each week would be a challenge, with no absolute guarantee of getting any money in.

"I was thinking," Stuart said. "Would the curtains from this house be of any use to you? They aren't long enough to fit the windows in the new house. You haven't got any plans for them, have you, Martha?" Stuart looked inquiringly at his wife.

"No, Penny is welcome to them, but I thought she'd want to choose her own."

"Thank you, they would do us a turn. I know Will is worried how we shall make out."

Penny was feeling just a little apprehensive. After all, they were burning their boats completely. There would be no going back now.

"Don't worry; Will is a hard-working chap. You will be okay. Besides, we shall be just down the road. So, you needn't go hungry." Martha smiled at her sister. There was a twinkle in her eye as she quipped, "True love will overcome all adversity."

At this, Penny threw a cushion at Martha, and they all laughed.

Then Stuart said, "Seriously, Penny, whatever problems you have, it's got to be better to share your life with someone you love than grow old on your own."

Next morning, Stuart gave Penny a lift to work.

"Isn't life great?" he said as he helped her down. "One minute, I thought we'd only see you occasionally. Now I find that you and Will will be practically next-door neighbours."

"Yes, it is wonderful," she agreed; there was a lightness in Penny's step as she went on her way. She was truly, happy.

Lizzie read the letter again, not really taking it all in at first. She was going to have to show it to Bill. First, she must be absolutely, clear what Penny was saying. She was very, attached to her. Somehow, she had always been able to share thoughts and feelings with her in a way she could not with her other two girls. But this was madness, surely. How much she must care to be willing to forsake everything for this man.

"Dear Mum and Dad," she read:

> This will take you by, surprise, but I have decided to accept Will's offer of marriage.
>
> There are a lot of things about Will I haven't told you. Like for instance that his mother is a Romany and that he has a son, Tim, who was born of a Sitka Indian woman. She nursed Will after an accident on the goldfields. This happened after he and I had lost touch. She died when the child was born. I intend to bring him up as my own son. He needs a loving home. We have been able to acquire a home and business only a short distance from where Martha and Stuart will be living. I would like to bring Will to meet you. I know you will like him. I have loved him for several years, and although I know we shall not be well off, at least to begin with, I feel sure we shall be happy. Please be glad for me. I know that when you get to know Will, you will realise what a good man he is.
>
> We shall be down on Friday night and return to London on Sunday afternoon.
>
> All my love,
> Penny

She carefully folded the letter and replaced it on the mantelpiece. Then she put the kettle on for tea and put Bill's slippers on the fender.

Presently, the familiar sound of boots being scraped, and an excited whimper of the dog, announced he was back from the field. She could hear him washing his hands ready for tea. He came into the room beaming.

"Hello, Lizzie," he said. "What kind of an afternoon have you had?"

"A letter came from Penny," she replied. "I don't know what to say about it."

He pulled on his slippers and lit his pipe. Then taking the letter from the mantelpiece, he unfolded it and began to read.

"Well, she is old enough to make up her own mind. But I can't say I'm not disappointed. Not only has he no position or money, but he is half-didicoi, with a child out of wedlock."

"When I think she could have had a good life with John Cooper and lived where we could have had the family around us, it makes me very sad." Lizzie was close to tears.

"That may be true, although we were a bit apprehensive about his gambling and drinking at the time." Bill puffed thoughtfully on the pipe. "One thing for sure: She will have a hard life now. But we mustn't,judge him before we meet him. Perhaps it won't be as bad as we fear."

As the week drew, to an end, Will was getting more and more nervous. How could he expect her parents to be pleased their daughter wanted to marry him? He would try not to let her down. He would wear a tie and a suit. He had bought some new socks and some Neat's foot oil to try and clear the squeak in his shoes. What was it they said about squeaky shoes not being paid for? He must be careful that Sally didn't pop his suit in the pawnbroker's; she'd do that sort of thing just to spite him. Why did she have to be like that about Penny? He had always been such good friends with his sister until now. Well, he reflected, she had a very, hard life. Perhaps it was making her bitter.

Penny had made up her mind and put aside all the worries about the visit home. Her busy life didn't give her time to brood; as usual, she was rushed off her feet on the wards.

She was on an early shift, and about midday, she made her way to the station clock, where she had arranged to meet Will. He was already there, looking tired and nervous. But as soon as he saw her, his face lit up with a smile.

"Pecker up," she said. "It won't be too terrible."

"How do you know?" he asked glumly.

"Because true love conquers all," she replied, laughing.

CHAPTER 12

Meeting the Future Parents-in-Law

ß & ß

It struck Will just how composed Penny was, seated opposite him in the carriage with her covered basket on the seat beside her. As she removed the pin from her large, brimmed hat, he thought how beautiful she was dressed and how readily a smile came to her lips. He was fortunate indeed.

As if responding to his thoughts, she took his hand and said, "We really are very lucky people."

"You won't change your mind if they don't approve of me, will you?" he asked earnestly.

"Well, I might if you look so solemn; I like a man with a bit of dash and daring."

Will laughed. "I might need plenty of that to face your father." He was still consumed with nerves, and the journey itself seemed to never end.

At last, the train pulled into Hastings Station. There was still a long wait before the carrier left George Street, so they made their way to the beach, where they sat among the pebbles and ate the sandwiches and fruit from Penny's basket. It was warm in the sun, with the distant sound of the surf. Children splashed and played in the rock pools. But it was just a brief interlude. The ordeal of facing Penny's parents was still to come.

It was early evening when they at last embarked on the journey by carrier from George Street; Penny was reminded of the journeys home. This time, life was once again changing for her.

As they sped along the Sussex countryside, she felt a great longing to stay. No other place touched her heart as this did, with its gentle rolling hills and red tiled farmhouses.

Will was very, quiet sitting beside her. Penny squeezed his hand and said softly, "Not far now."

The carrier smiled; he had known Penny all her life. "Taking you home to meet the family, is she?" With a flick at the reins, he went on, "Bill Thompson isn't as fierce as he looks. But Lizzie is a grand little lady. You'll be alright."

Will had to laugh. "Thanks," he said. "That gives me great courage."

Shortly, they drew up at the cottage gate. The door was flung open, and Lizzie Thompson stood there, her arms outstretched to hug her daughter.

"I heard you coming. Have you had a good journey?"

Before she could answer, her father came to the door.

"Glad you made it alright."

Will was awestruck, for he was confronted by this huge man, who towered over him by at least nine inches, broad chested with thick bushy eyebrows, piercing blue eyes, and the biggest crop of whiskers he had ever seen.

His wife was tiny and petite, but Lizzie's handshake was firm, and her brown eyes held a warmth that immediately made him feel at ease.

"Come on in. I'll put the kettle on." Lizzie was not keen on the match, but she would make a welcome for Penny's sake.

Later, while the women cleared the dishes, Will accompanied her father around his market garden.

Secretly, Penny hoped that Will was not getting too much of a grilling from her father. She need not have worried, for when they returned, they were obviously getting on like a house on fire.

"This young chap has certainly got some good ideas for the smallholding," Bill said, taking out his pipe and rolling a plug of tobacco. "I think you will do well, providing the railway doesn't take too much of your trade."

This was the first time anyone had raised any doubts as to the viability of the carrier business. Will knew he had made a good impression on his future father-in-law with his ideas for the holding. But it was crucial that the carrying business was profitable; for the first time, Will had a nagging doubt if he was doing the right thing.

But first things first, he told himself; he still had to convince her mother that he'd be a good husband.

But Will was an affable young man, and by the time they left on Sunday, Lizzie had decided that if he was what Penny wanted, she would not try to change her mind. After all, she might grow to like him.

Jane was delighted to hear Penny's news. She had never blamed her for what John Cooper had done to Jason by calling in the loan. In fact, she told her mother how pleased she was that Penny had not married such a hard man.

"Will seems a kind person; that's what really counts, isn't it? Love and kindness."

Her mother smiled. Heaven knows, she thought, Jane's husband has shown plenty of that. Now she seems so much better, and their boy Peter had filled out and lost that transparent look. Hopefully, the consumption had left their family for good.

"Yes, you are quite right, Jane; a kind man is the best partner for any woman. It all seems to be turning out well, although I can't think it will be anything but hard work for Penny. But as long, as she is happy, that's the main thing."

"Well," Jane replied, "Jason soon learnt to be a market gardener; he wouldn't want to go back to farming now. So perhaps he will be just as successful as a carrier."

"Perhaps it's a good thing Penny called off her wedding to John Cooper. His gambling and drinking ways have returned by all accounts. But she broke his heart, and he married on the rebound. It was very sad."

"It's no good dwelling on the past. I think they will be very happy." Jane at least was convinced. "Must be going on my way now, I am doing the altar flowers today." She gave her mum a quick reassuring hug, picked up her bag and coat, and left the house.

Lizzie could hear her humming as she strolled down the path. The young ones had great resilience, she realised. They were not beset with doubt as she was. Would she never stop worrying about her children?

CHAPTER 13

Will Leaves Sally's House, Taking Tim to His Parents

B ack in London, Will still had to break the news to Sally. He had always realised that she was likely to voice her opposition. But even he was not, prepared for the pure vitriol that poured over him as he walked in. Her face contorted with rage, she started shouting," Where the hell have you been?" Without even waiting for his answer she went on. "I suppose you have been with, her, you needn't think I'm going to shoulder your responsibilities while you are off gallivanting about with her. You can get out and take your little redskin with you."

She continued to lash at him with her tongue. But Will was no longer listening. He had had enough. Packing his few possessions and what clothes he could find for Tim into a bag. He lifted the sleeping child and departed.

The horse snorted at being disturbed in the night, but Will methodically set to work putting on the harness and attaching the cart. Tim who was asleep in the hay stirred as his father lifted him into the cart, laying him on a bed of hay. With a flick of the reins, they were off.

Breakfast was in progress at the nurses' home when the doorbell rang. Someone called out, "Telegram for Penny Thompson."

She could hardly believe her ears. Thoughts of disaster crowded her mind.

"Here, let me see," she heard herself say.

"Meet me at Uxbridge station, Saturday afternoon, Will."

She told the messenger to reply, "I will be there, three o'clock train, Penny."

She could not help wondering what on earth had happened. It stayed on her mind all week. Usually, when she was off duty, Will would meet her and spend the evening with her. But this week, there was no sign of him. Could it be he had cold feet now that they had decided to marry? Or had the agreement with Jim Logan failed? Certainly, if that had happened, their plans were in ruins. She tried not to think of it, throwing herself wholeheartedly into her work.

As the train pulled into Uxbridge station, she could see Will pacing up and down the platform. His face lit up with a smile as he caught sight of her.

"Sorry to have frightened you with the telegram," he said after he had given her a kiss and a hug. "But I couldn't think of any other way to let you know I had left Sally's place in a hurry. Tim's with Mum and Dad."

"But why?" Penny asked.

"Let's go and have a cup of tea, then I can tell you all about it."

At last, seated in the tea shop with a pot of tea and a plate of cakes, Will explained that Sally had taken the news of his leaving badly. Penny wasn't surprised. She had always felt Sally's hostility towards her. Also, the money Will contributed to the household was vital. With a sick husband and four children to support, she would be worried.

"What will she do?" Penny asked.

"Well, she could foster another child or take in a lodger," Will replied. "I didn't promise to do it for a lifetime, you know."

"I know that. But it's hard all the same." Penny felt sorry for Sally. But she knew she had made an enemy. *Thank heavens I get on well with his parents,* she thought.

"Do you want to hear my other news, then?"

"Of course, I do."

"Dad has lent me the down payment on James Logan's place. I have already started learning the ropes with him this week. I've met the customers and am learning how to be on time and meet the trains and work out the return loads, you know."

"Why, that is wonderful news." She hadn't expected this; it was all moving ahead so quickly.

"We could set the date now," he added. "But I think we should see how the business goes first, don't you?"

Will sounded hesitant as he spoke. He had little money to fall back on; no doubt Penny earned more than he did, and he was asking her to give it all up to live with him and care for Tim.

"Does your mum mind, having him for a few months?" Penny asked. "I was thinking of saving a little more first; Stuart and Martha are moving into their place in August. The baby is due in September, so what do you think? Should we make it December? Although I want Martha to come, and she may not want to travel with a baby in winter."

Will was smiling as Penny rattled on.

"I've got a better idea," he replied. "How about getting married on Boxing Day? It's free at our local church. We could have a reception in our own house. There would be plenty of room. You could stay with Martha and Stuart beforehand. Your parents can stay in our house. How does that sound?"

Will looked so pleased with himself, Penny had to laugh.

"I believe you've already worked it all out. We will have to see what Mum and Dad say. They may want it to be at home. But it will be better for Martha and the baby not to travel."

"That's settled, then; let's have another cuppa. Then we had better go; we're expected for tea, and Mum will be getting anxious. But I'm glad we had a chance to chat first. It seems difficult to get any time on our own these days. I was worried you'd think I was rushing things."

"Well, you are, aren't you?" Penny laughed at his response. "I'm glad," she said, squeezing his hand.

Eliza was anxiously waiting for Will and Penny. If they were coming to tea, they were very late.

"I tell you, he has gone too far this time," she told her husband. "Making all those decisions without asking her first. I just hope he hasn't put her off, that's all.

Bill drew on his pipe, reflecting that he hoped all was well. Minding young Tim while Will got himself sorted out was one thing; showing him the poultry and taking him on fishing trips was fun for Grandad. But at this time in their life, neither he nor Eliza wanted the responsibility of bring him up for good. He could see how tired Eliza was. After all, they had brought up seven of their own.

"They'll be alright," he said without mentioning what was on his mind. "Don't worry."

"Hello," Will called. "Sorry we're late."

He looked at Eliza, and she gave a sigh of relief.

"There," he said, getting up from his chair. "What did I tell you?"

Eliza pretended not to hear.

"Fetch Tim in," she said, "and see he washes his hands."

CHAPTER 14

From Martha's Home to Curlew Cottage

B B B

"I've been thinking," Stuart said, laying down his fork and looking across the table at Penny. "Would you like to come and work for me for a few months? Martha is going to have her hands full with the baby, and frankly, I could use some help getting the files straight and manning the fort while I am out on my rounds. What do you think? You could also give Martha a hand sorting out the move."

Stuart had been mulling this idea over for some time. He was frankly worried that he would be too busy with the new practice to give Martha the support she would need. Moving was going to be traumatic enough without a new job and a new baby on the way.

Martha was aghast that he'd even suggest such a thing. "You can't ask her to do that," she said. "It's too much for anyone. The poor girl would be worn to a frazzle."

"No, wait a minute, Martha." Penny smiled at her sister. "It could be the answer for me. But only until Christmas. By that time, you could help Stuart and hire a girl to help with the house and the baby."

"Why Christmas?" Stuart asked.

"Because that is when we're going to be married. At least that's the plan at the moment. I haven't discussed it with Mum and Dad yet. So, it's not definite."

"But what made you choose December?" Martha asked.

"Well, it's a long story. I wanted you at the wedding, but I was worried about travelling in the winter with a baby. Will wants to get married soon. Partly because his parents are having to care for Tim, and also because we already have the house and business. Will had this idea that we could have the wedding locally. If you could put up with me, I could stay here. Mum, Dad, and the family could stay at our place."

"It sounds a good idea to me. You could prepare the reception in our kitchen. Mum could stay, and we could all help."

Martha was quite excited. It looked as though everything was about to work out fine. Soon, she would be settled in a new home, with Penny to help. For this, she was deeply thankful. This late in her pregnancy, she felt increasingly tired and clumsy. It had worried her how she would cope. Penny, for her part, couldn't believe how quickly her life was to change. It was unbelievable that she should have such good luck.

Back at the hospital, Penny felt almost tearful on her last day. She had resided at the nurses' home for so long, it felt like leaving her family. Staff and patients had a whip round and presented her with a china tea service and a large bouquet of flowers. Smiling but with tears in her eyes, she thanked everyone and told them she would miss them all. Later that day, she collected her things and took a cab to Martha's. They had just two days to prepare for the move. Penny had been popping in whenever she had time and packing things into tea chests. So apart from the things in daily use, most of the packing had been done.

On the day of the move, it was unbearably hot, and Martha, now in the eighth month of her pregnancy, was so overcome by it that as soon as the beds were installed in the new home, she had to lay down. Stuart was very, concerned for her.

"I'm so glad you agreed to help us," he said to Penny. "I'm afraid it was all too much for Martha so late in her pregnancy. Unfortunately, that's the way the timing of the job fell. Mind you, if I had known it would be this hot, I would have changed the date."

"You go and sit with Martha while I find my way around the kitchen," she said. "I'll get a bite to eat once I can lay my hands on the picnic hamper. There it is!"

After she grabbed the hamper, she retrieved the kettle, lit the stove, and made a pot of tea; she prepared a light meal of ham salad and crusty rolls with butter. Martha managed very, little to eat. She had a few sips of tea and then lay down again. Penny washed her face gently and put a cool pad on her forehead.

"I do hope it's only exhaustion," Stuart said, clearly worried. "Perhaps she will feel better after a sleep."

After supper, Penny looked in on Martha, who was asleep.

"I think I'll turn in now," she said. Goodnight, Stuart."

"I shall do the same," he replied. "Goodnight."

Hardly had Penny's eyes closed when she heard Stuart moving in the kitchen. He was restocking the fire and filling kettles with water. She quickly dressed and went to see what was happening.

"Sorry I disturbed you," Stuart said. "Martha has started her contractions."

"Leave that," she replied. "I will see to things here while you go for Dr Millard and the midwife."

Stuart nodded. "Yes, I don't think it will be here yet. But I had better let them know."

He disappeared into the night, and Penny went in to see how Martha was. She had a better colour than she had a few hours before, and she seemed quite cheerful.

"I am going to get it all over at once," she said between contractions.

Penny smiled. "You're a glutton for punishment: moving house,and having a baby on the same day."

After what seemed an eternity, Stuart returned with the midwife. Dr Millard had been out, but his wife was getting a message to him. Penny, meanwhile, was sorting out the linen, getting the baby things ready, and boiling plenty of water. She had not had time to unpack yet.

"If the pace of life here continues at this rate," she said, "we shall all be worn to a frazzle. You certainly don't waste time." She turned from her sister to smile at the midwife. "She didn't even wait for an introduction to you before fetching you out."

The midwife, who was about the same age as Martha, laughed.

"Good job all my ladies aren't in such a hurry."

As it turned out, it was some hours before the cries of a, newborn, baby were heard. He had lusty lungs and weighed in at eight pounds.

During the next month, life was very hectic. Stuart was now on call, although Martha remained rather weak after the birth. Gradually, Penny got the household running well. There was more work helping with the practice than they had realised, so a young girl from the village came to help Martha with the baby. Penny was at last able to spend the evenings and Sunday afternoons helping Will to get their home ready. The curtains from Martha's London home had been adapted, and they added some furniture to the few pieces Jim Logan had left. Will had done the more pressing repairs, and together, they had given the whole place a fresh coat of paint before the weather broke.

At the end of October, they went to see the parson to arrange the reading of the banns. Her parents had gone along with the arrangement. Penny was glad. Banns were not going to be read at home, for she had never discussed her engagement to John Cooper. She had decided that there was nothing to be gained by dragging up the past.

Each day now, she would call round at her future in-laws,house to collect young Tim for a walk. The young lad would run ahead, kicking the fallen leaves and throwing sticks for his grandfather's dog. He had lost his shyness with her now. Together, they shared many adventures and much laughter. For Penny, this meant she could once again see things through the eyes of a child, and it brought her great joy.

When Will saw them together, he knew that all was, well. His fear that they would not get on was groundless. Yet he still had a gnawing doubt that Jim Logan's business was insufficient to pay off the loan and keep the family as well. He grew preoccupied, until one day, Penny asked, "Are you having second thoughts?"

"Of course not," he replied. "What makes you say a thing like that?"

"It's just that you seem so quiet and far away in your thoughts. Is something wrong?"

"Well, yes, there is." He struggled to find the right words. "I don't think there is enough coming in to keep us and pay off the loan. I don't know a solution to the problem yet, but I'm working on it."

"We'll find a way. We always knew it would be a tight struggle." She smiled at him reassuringly.

"But I don't want you to have to take in lodgers. I want to be the one to support my family." Having had his say, he relapsed into silence and got on with his painting.

Later that evening, Penny decided to ask Stuart if she could continue working as his receptionist after the wedding. Although he couldn't afford to pay her much, anything extra might help to bridge the gap. But when she approached Stuart, he wasn't so sure.

"You know I'd be delighted to have you stay," he said, "but what about Will? He may not want you to work after your marriage. I don't want to cause a rift."

"If you would ask him if I could help you out, I'm sure he wouldn't object."

Stuart laughed. "You're a devious lady; isn't she, Martha?"

His wife looked amused and said, "I don't know about devious; more a survivor, I think."

CHAPTER 15

Winter Blues

⌐ ⌐ ⌐

November came in, dank and foggy. But in spite, of the awful weather, Will's spirits were high. Now that Stuart asked Penny to continue to help in the practice, he was no longer worried about the shortage of money. He was feeling confident he could make a go of the business. He recently landed a contract to carry coal from the canal wharf at Denham to the local coal merchant. He knew it was seasonal, but at least it meant he could put a little money aside for a rainy day.

Collecting the coal from the wharf was arduous work. The barge would come alongside the wharf with a butty boat behind. As the coal was unloaded, Will had to weigh it off in sacks on the canal company's weighing machine. Then with the help of a mate, the bags were loaded onto his cart. Then began the journey back to the coal merchant's yard in the village.

Sometimes, he took a whole load directly to a customer. Other times, he had to offload it onto a flat trolley, ready for the coal merchant to deliver later. It was hard work, and it didn't take Will long to see that he was making most of the effort while the coal merchant made a good living. The coal merchant had solved the problem of seasonal work by also being the local wood merchant. Two men worked sawing planks in the pit in his yard. It was gruelling work with a two-handed saw, one man below the other on the platform above.

Also, in the yard was a steam kiln to season the wood. Some of these were made into coffins by a jobbing carpenter. Standing in the corner now were spare ones in three sizes.

"After he has worn you out, he'll fit you up in one of those," the sawyers joked.

"Well, you've got to hand it to him; he doesn't miss a trick."

After work, he rubbed down the horse and cleaned the tack and cart. He thought a lot about what he had seen at the coal yard and came to the conclusion that you either found something to buy and sell that people needed, or you spent your whole life doing grinding, hard work, like he was doing now. But for the moment, he must be content. One day, he meant to make his mark in the business world.

Will and his father had many conversations about this; Thomas was always in favour of caution.

"You need a lot of capital to do any good," he would say. "Bad debt can ruin you."

But Will only laughed the good advice off.

"Think big, act big, and you will be big," he would say.

"Think big, act big, and be bankrupt, more like," his father would retort.

But at least for the moment, it was only talk.

Penny was trying on the dress and jacket her mother had made for the wedding. It was made of dark green velvet, edged with black fur at the neck and bottom of the jacket, with a large, brimmed hat trimmed with the same black fur. The long sweep of the skirt swished about the new black button boots, and a black fur muff completed the ensemble.

"You look lovely. It does suit you so. You look quite the lady." Martha, who hadn't got her figure back yet, sounded wistful.

"I thought so too," Penny said, sounding pleased. "Mum is such a good needlewoman; just look at the work she has put into this jacket."

Just at that moment, Stuart came into the room. "What's this, then," he asked. "A fashion, show?" He glanced approvingly at Penny's outfit. "This is for the great day, I take it?"

"Yes, isn't it a lovely choice?"

Stuart, looking at his is sister-in-law in her finery, knew she was indeed a brave girl. He saw plenty of girls like Penny struggling to keep a good home on a pittance. Most found it too hard and aged before their time. But she looked so happy and confident that he felt sure she'd make life what she wanted it to be.

"You look beautiful, Penny; nearly as lovely as your sister."

Stuart smiled at Martha, and Penny thought how happy those two are, and she hoped that she and Will would be as lucky.

The wedding took place in the local church. There were two other couples taking advantage of the free Boxing Day service, and the church was filled with friends and families of all three couples. It was a very, happy affair. The choir knew them all and had come along to give their best for their friends. Afterwards, they all walked back to their home for refreshments, many of them reappearing at Will's barn, where they had dance to the fiddle and concertina of two village lads. It was a grand party attended by most of the village. The squire turned up with two casks of cider and joined in the dancing. By morning, there were more than a few sore heads.

Penny's parents, Jane, and Peter stayed with Martha and Stuart for a few days' rest before returning home.

Now Lizzie knew exactly where her two oldest girls were; she had met their friends and seen that they were happy.

"It looks as if it may turn out well, after all," she told Bill. "At least Penny will have Martha and Stuart close by."

"Do stop worrying," he replied. "They'll make out the same as we had to. After all, they know what they are taking on."

But he wondered if they actually did. Haulage was very dependent on others, and the rail was, very competitive. Paying back a loan was going to take some doing too. But in the end, he reasoned they had to find out for themselves.

The holiday soon ended. The morning of their departure was frosty. Penny, Will, Stuart, and Martha travelled to Uxbridge to see them off on the first stage of the journey back to Sussex. Penny shed a few tears as she waved goodbye, partly because home, among the fields and by the seashore, was now firmly in the past. It felt like the final parting from her old life.

Shaking herself out of the reverie, she turned to her sister and asked, "Shall we just go for a cup of tea before we go home?"

Martha wasn't fooled by this. "You can always go home to stay, you know," she said. "Mum and Dad would want you to visit whenever you could."

"Of course," Will said. "Go whenever you want." He hoped Penny would grow to like his home as much as she was attached to her own.

Stuart felt the tension of the station farewells and suggested they go for a cup of tea anyway, as he needed it. Badly.

"Come on, then," Martha said gaily. "He is suffering from shock. Hot sweet tea is what he needs."

"Why?" Will asked. "What have you been up to then, Martha?"

"You might well ask," Stuart replied. "She bought a dog because she felt sorry for it, and it has chewed the leg off the kitchen table. I came down this morning, made a pot of tea, stood it on the table, and it fell off. Everything fell off. What a mess; you know how unconscious I am when I first get up."

Will was laughing. "What are you going to do with the dog?"

"Oh, don't you know? Tim brought him back to your place, said it would keep intruders out of the barn."

Will could hardly contain himself. "That's a wooden barn, you know."

"Yes," Stuart replied drolly. "He's probably demolished it by now."

They all laughed at the expression on Will's face. Penny was happy again. Wasn't it grand, she thought, that the four of them got on so well? There would be plenty of laughs and fun together in the years ahead.

The two sisters made their way to the tea shop, Will and Stuart talking behind them.

"I am very glad you decided to take Jim Logan up on his offer," Stuart said.

"I hope it was the right decision, that's all," Will replied.

"Surely not regretting married life already."

"No. Nothing like that. But it is a worry having a loan and not being sure if you can make a go of it."

"Well, at least you will have the satisfaction of knowing you tried," Stuart said, knowing the platitude he offered sounded hollow; he had never had to make his way from scratch. His parents had been able to afford to pay for his training, and as a professional man, money was not a crucial worry.

The two women were already seated at the table when they walked in, laughing together.

"They seem confident enough, anyway," Stuart remarked to Will.

"Come on, you two," Martha said. "We are waiting to order. I am famished."

"What's it to be, then?" Stuart asked. "Toasted tea cakes and a pot of tea?"

Now that the honeymoon was over and Christmas had past, Tim came from his grandparents to live at Curlew cottage.

The old gander and his wife had been fenced out of the garden and grazed with the horses and two cows in the paddock. Will divided their few acres to rotate their grazing. But for this first year, they had to buy hay and roots for the stock. Another year, they hoped to grow more vegetables too, as there were only a few sprouts and some broccoli planted by Jim Logan. He hadn't needed much on his own.

The winter was long and severe. There were many days when Will could not work, and their slender resources were shrinking alarmingly. Will's parents took to dropping by, bringing gifts of a few eggs, vegetables from the garden, a bag of potatoes, and bottled fruit. Martha too would bring half a chicken or cold beef, saying they had more than they needed. Will felt it keenly and was very upset that he couldn't provide enough for his family.

"It will be alright in the spring," his father told him. "You'll have the calves, if you need to sell them, and I have some good pullets for you; they should start producing eggs to sell in February. Once you get the vegetables, eggs, and poultry bringing something in, you will find things picking up."

But building up the business was harder than Will had anticipated; most things seem to grind to a halt with the freezing weather.

Young Tim had lost his city pallor, and he and Penny would feed the stock and then take the sledge to play on the slopes. They seemed oblivious to Will's worries. Every day, Penny produced a substantial hot meal and never seemed worried or out of humour. She and Tim planned where they would plant seeds when spring came. As for Will, he came to feel that winter would never end.

Then at last, it warmed up, and the snow and ice turned to slush and rain. Will was able to start the haulage again. Driving with a sack around his shoulders to keep off the worst of the wet, he felt he was always damp and clammy. But with silver in his pocket again, he soon cheered up.

In February, there was a spell of warm weather, and they were able to prepare the soil for the vegetables. This at least felt like progress. The sun seemed to awaken the sleeping plants and trees. The sap could be seen rising in the trees, and the gander became really aggressive again. His two wives started to lay larger eggs than Tim had ever seen.

"We'll soon have some goslings," Will told him.

But Penny decided to take the first eggs to make omelettes and egg custard tarts. Just one was enough to make scrambled egg for three of them.

March came in like a lion, blowing down several trees. But the geese, who were by now sitting in their nests and about to hatch a clutch of eggs, did not bat an eyelid at the weather. Penny and Tim spent hours gathering fallen branches for kindling. Will and his father set to and sawed the rest into logs. *At least,* Penny thought to herself, *we shall have firewood next winter.*

Will now had a contract to haul lime from the canals to the squire's tenant farmers. The squire had known Will as a boy and tried to put work his way whenever he could. Things remained very tight, however, and when Penny told Will she thought she was pregnant, he knew he should be glad, but he wasn't. All he could think was, another mouth to feed.

"I could take in two working men as lodgers just until things pick up," Penny suggested, watching Will carefully to see his reaction.

He sighed and said, "Alright, but you'll have to give up helping Stuart; you can't do it all. I'm the one who has to find a way to make ends meet."

He blamed himself being for being such an optimist. He ought to have got the business going before dragging Penny into such grinding poverty. *God knows how I'm going to sort it out,* he thought to himself.

Now at the end of the day, Will returned home to find the two lodgers relaxing by his fireside. It was difficult to find any privacy at all. Whereas before, he had stripped off in the kitchen to wash, now, he found himself washing in the boiler house or using a jug and bowl on the bedroom washstand. There was never a moment to talk privately with Penny, unless they were in the privacy of their bedroom.

One evening, depressed by the unending grind, on a day that had been worse than usual, Will decided to stop off at a pub for just one pint. He knew as soon as he returned home, Penny would ask him what sort of day he had, and he just couldn't face telling her how awful it was. As he was about to order, a half-drunk Irishman at the bar called out to him, "What'll you have, my friend?"

"Thanks all the same. I'll get my own," Will replied gruffly.

"Oh, come on. I've plenty, and there's more where this came from."

The man pulled out a roll of banknotes from his hip pocket. It was years since Will had set eyes on such a lot of money.

"Where'd you get it?" he asked incredulously.

"Oh, me and my mates are digging like bloody moles under London. Building the London underground railway."

"Any chance of getting in on a good thing like that?"

"They want some strong chaps next week. The muck has to be carted out to Blackheath Common. It's night shift, but you'll have to be sharp if you want to join." Just give me the address and the name of the company and I will see you at work.I am so pleased to have met you." Raising his glass he drained his pint and waved cheerio and set off for, home, his spirits lifted .

Will decided to have a go; his capital was all but exhausted, as indeed he knew Penny was. He had seen her on Monday stoking the copper, boiling sheets, shirts, and towels. He saw the strain in her face as she stooped and then brushed the hair from her eyes, already traces of grey showing.

I have to do something drastic, he told himself. *We can't go on like this for another year.*

When he returned home, he called her into the kitchen. "Penny, I want you to send a telegram to your parents," he said. "Tell them you and Tim are coming to stay for a while. It will be a good time to tell them about the baby."

"But I can't do that," she said. "Who will look after the lodgers? And what about you?"

"I'll see to that. You go and have a rest."

Penny guessed he was up to something, but she was feeling so weary that she did as he asked.

Will saw them off at the station. It was a gamble. He knew he was throwing away the goodwill that Jim Logan had built up over the years, as well as the contracts and contacts he himself had worked for, but it was not generating enough money to keep them. There was a very real possibility of going bankrupt if he had another quiet spell this winter.

Feeling more cheerful now that he had decided to do something positive, he set off to the horse fair to sell his horse and cart. Tonight, he would give the lodgers notice. Then he would tell his parents what he was up to. He didn't relish doing that, worried that his dad would feel let down because he had loaned him the money for the down payment. But it had to be faced up to.

In the event, the old man took the news quietly. "What will you do when the railway is finished, though?" he asked.

"Hopefully, another door will open," Will replied.

His father sucked thoughtfully on his pipe. He himself had stuck with the same job for many years. Providing for seven children which meant curbing his ambitions. He had never felt able to risk everything to get on. But he hadn't done badly, he reflected. He had been foreman for several years before he retired.

"Well, you must do as you think fit," he said. "I'll look after the stock while Penny is away."

"Thanks," Will replied. "I'm very grateful to you and Mum; sorry that it didn't work out."

CHAPTER 16

Underground

ß ℰ ß

The wet clay streaked down Will's sweat-stained face. Clawing his way along the narrow tunnels on his belly, he heaved the heavy pit props into position and hacked at the seemingly endless sticky grey mud. London clay, they called it, and very unstable it was too, oozing out of shape even as he set the props up. This was hell on earth.

He loaded the spoil into small trucks, which others winched up to the surface. From there, it was taken to Blackheath and spread on the common. Next week, it would be his turn to spread it. It was, no doubt, just as hard as a job, but at least he'd be able to straighten his back for a few days.

He slept in a crude shelter along with the other navvies, for that was what the people called them. But the pay was good. Unlike his companions, Will neither played cards nor drank to excess, saving every penny he could.

Penny, who had now returned home, saw little of him even at the weekends, for as soon as he was washed and had eaten, he would fall into an exhausted stupor.

"Will, you can't go on like this," she said one day, standing over him with a cup of tea. "You are killing yourself.

Will pull himself up on his pillow and said, "Time to go again, is it? I'm alright; just give me six months then we can start again."

Things were certainly looking up in financial terms. But Penny was struggling on at home, feeding the chickens and milking the cows; it was getting more difficult for her as her pregnancy advanced. True, Tim was starting school in September, but she knew she'd be unable to carry on milking and weeding.

She had grown so much produce that she regularly brought eggs, vegetables, and flowers to market. Will's father came by with his trap to take her to market every Tuesday. She also made butter from surplus milk and fed the whey to the pigs. They were self-sufficient in so many ways, but they still had to buy feed stuff for the animals.

Martha was getting very worried that her sister was overworked.

"What can Will be thinking of, leaving her all week to do all the work?" she asked Stuart.

"I think," he replied, "that Will is trying to avoid becoming bankrupt."

"Do you really think it is as bad as that?"

"Yes, and do you know that what Will is doing? He is tearing his gut, on his hands and knees, tunnelling under London."

Martha was deeply shocked.

"Oh, my goodness. And to think we encouraged them to take it on."

"Well, don't underestimate their tenacity. If he can stick it out, they should weather the storm."

"But what about Penny? She can't carry on without help. I shall have to help milk the cows and do the weeding."

Stuart smiled. "Yes, but I suppose I could employ a girl from the village to mind our child. Surely it would be better to get the gardener to call there in the morning, milk the cows, do two hours on the vegetable patch, and then come to us."

"Do you think he would? That would solve the problem, wouldn't it?"

He smiled at Martha and thought what a lucky fellow he was to have married such a kind person. He had no intention of letting her take on too much. It had taken some months for her to regain her health after the birth of their baby.

The next week, Stuart spoke to Will about his suggestion. Will was obviously pleased with the idea. "Do you think he would be willing to do it? I have to,admit I have been worried sick, wondering what to do. The job doesn't finish until a month after the baby comes. Penny's mum is coming up to mind young Tim and help with the baby. But the animals and the garden are a worry. My dad could feed the birds, but at his age, it isn't fair to ask him to do the milking too."

"Well, I'll have a word with the gardener on Monday and see what we can arrange."

Will felt a great weight had been lifted from him. He knew he could give the job up now, and probably should, to be with Penny. But he was ambitious, and the thought of accumulating more capital drove him on. He meant to have another try at business, but this time, he'd have the resources to cushion him through the lean times.

CHAPTER 17

Tim Learns It's a Man's World

W ill did not always get home for the weekends. The cold wet weather had put the work schedule behind, and everyone was pushing ahead relentlessly. The thick clay caused many problems. In some places, tunnels had to be opened up, making high embankments. Accidents became common. Discontent with their lot was spreading among the navvies. But Will battled on, confident that he would soon have his capital. Next year, this line would be open.

Time marched on, and for Penny, there seldom seemed a moment to call her own. For Will, it was the last months of opportunity to earn good money.

He began to look around and keep his ear to the ground for either another job or an opening to start in business again. A recruiter from the Amalgamated Society of Railway Servants talked to the navvies one evening, which helped him decide which way to go. This recruiter had been talking about the discontent among the railway workers, saying that if they decided to have a national railway strike, it would disrupt the transport of goods so severely that the navvies would be bound to get pay rises.

Will knew that in some areas, rail workers had their wages reduced rather than raised. He puzzled about this as he lay in his bunk between shifts. If he obtained a good coal wharf, he could be a coal merchant, with the coal delivered by canal. He had some experience of this from his carrier days.

The seed of an idea was sown. It would need to be nearer to a bigger conurbation. His thoughts travelled on. It needed to be somewhere that relied on the rail supplies. But it seemed to him that the discontent spreading a strike could be to his advantage. He just could not wait to discuss it with Penny.

Penny heard him out and then said, to Will's surprise, "Yes, I agree. Everyone needs coal, but what about this place? We owe your father the initial loan, and there are still payments to make to Jim Logan."

"Well, we could sell up here and pay them off, then, if need be, refinance the business."

But Penny did not look convinced; he would have to work out how it could be done, find a place, and then discuss it with her again.

For her part, Penny was afraid that they might lose all they had sacrificed so much for.

Will dropped the subject for the moment; he was still looking for an opening into something else. Now with less than two months before the line opened, it became a nagging worry. Some of the navvies were moving on to repairing and dredging sections of the canals; pay was poor and conditions equally as dangerous as they had been digging the underground railway. But lacking any alternative, he decided to apply for a job. Dressed smartly with a collar and tie and well-polished boots, he presented himself at the district superintendent's office. The interview went well, although Will did think some of the questions strange for a navvy's job.

The superintendent finished writing in his book. Then he looked up and said, "Well, young man, I am giving you the job; you will have a rent-free cottage and twelve shillings per week. One more thing; do you have children?"

"A son, sir; he is just learning to crawl."

"Well, in that case, just take care to keep him away from the water."

Hardly able to comprehend what had happened, Will found to his surprise that he had applied on the day a new linesman was to be appointed. Now he would be caring for a set of locks and the length of bank that went with them. He was so excited. This would give him the security he needed; he could always reassess the opportunities when they arose.

When he got home, he pushed the door of Curlew cottage open and called out, "What do you think I'm going to be? A linesman."

"A what?" Penny asked.

"A linesman."

Penny just could not believe her ears. "But how did you hear about that job? I thought you were going for dredging and repairing."

"So did I; it was an amazing stroke of luck."

"I'm glad you wore a collar and tie."

"Yes, and polished my shoes."

His smile grew larger when he told her of the rent- free cottage. "Now we can sell up here; think of it, no more debt."

Penny was excited. A settled life at last, she thought. Will still had his ambitions, but for the moment, they were on hold.

It did not take long to sell Curlew cottage, for in their time, they had improved both the inside and out. The fences were in good shape, gardens were well stocked, and there was good stabling and storage. A retired farmer took it on. Unable to face giving up entirely, he was glad to take on the geese, some hens, and the cows as well.

Penny knew she would miss the home they had made; despite all the hardships, she had enjoyed her first home with Will, Tim, and the new baby, Michael. Now they were on the move to a new life. One consolation was that they would still be close to Martha, Stuart, and their son John, and not far from Will's parents.

Will was concerned about what his father would think, but he need not have worried. Bill Thompson was delighted by his son's news. He knew that despite the gruelling hard work, Will had not been able to make the carrier business profitable. Working on the underground had been as hazardous a job as going down mines. He had often blamed himself for loaning Will the deposit to buy out Jim Logan, for he felt they had been overstretched financially ever since.

Now with a regular job and house, he hoped they would be settled and comfortable.

The move took place over the following weekend. The goods and chattels were loaded on a hired cart, but the horse was so old that they had to make several trips, including a crate of hens and two piglets from the old sow's litter.

The cottage had two bedrooms and a box room, living room, parlour, small kitchen, and an outside privy, pigsty, and a fuel store in a walled in square. The garden was large and overgrown, with a sad-looking damson tree, cankerous plum, and overgrown gooseberry bushes. Penny had lifted many plants for her new garden. Caring for them and working to get the garden under control was a nightmare, especially as Michael was now beginning to crawl, and the perimeter fence was rotten.

Will was very busy cutting reeds and grass with a scythe, clearing the waterway of obstructions, servicing the lock gates, and adjusting water levels.

One day, Harry Barber, the superintendent, paid an unexpected visit. Penny took to him on sight. He was a lovely man with a kind twinkle in his eye.

"I want a word with you, young man," he said to Will.

Apprehensive, Will said, "Well, come in, sir; you can have a word with me over a cup of tea."

Penny hastily set the cups and some ginger snaps on a tray. As she did so, she heard laughter coming from the room. What a relief, she thought; nothing was seriously wrong then.

As she bustled in with the tea, Mr Barber spoke to her: "I've been telling your husband to leave everything for a day or two and get the garden fence secure against this young man. Little Michael is too young to learn to swim, and the locks are dangerous places at the best of times. A load of posts and rails are being delivered this afternoon, together with a roll of netting."

He waved aside their thanks and said, "It is my duty to look after our staff. It really should have been seen to before you moved in. But we were overstretched, owing to a breach last month."

After he had gone, Penny suggested they have an early lunch.

"If there are a lot of posts to unload, you might not get a chance to eat until late," she said, and Will agreed.

This was certainly going to be a big help being supplied with all he needed to fence the garden; perhaps it wasn't so bad being a tenant. But he knew keeping his home depended on how well the superintendent thought he did his job. Fortunately, thanks to the underground railway, they had money for a rainy day. He didn't think that was a worry at the moment, but what if the superintendent left? He might find a new man would want him out for one of his family or friends. It was by no means as secure as all that.

Tim helped his father with the fencing after school. Though he was only seven, he was big for his age and loved to help. He would hold the post straight for Will to get it started, and when at last they started to put the wire around the finished fence, he passed the staples to his father and pulled the wire tight.

Will often rose early to get the grass cutting done before the heat of the day became too much. Throughout the first summer, he met many of the boatman and their families. Most now lived aboard the barges, as their rates of pay had been pared down to such a degree that they could no longer maintain a land-based home. For many children, this meant missing school .Tim had been a victim of bullying at school,Will had taken his son outside and taught him how to box, and evade the blows aimed at him.

Most of the boats took coal one way and returned with loads of wood, iron, and other manufactured goods. Many were still pulled by horses that, after many years, walked with a sideways gait.

Tim now had a stream of constantly changing friends, children of the bargees, whose countenance was as dark as his, and so he no longer felt different, and the fighting ceased.

. He learnt to paint the gaily painted castles and roses, and helped his friends clean the brasses.

By the end of the first year, Penny was selling the surplus fruit and vegetables at the market again; they were still producing their own pork, bacon, chicken, and eggs.

The next year also progressed well; the garden produce was in abundance. Penny could just not believe their luck: a regular wage and plenty to eat.

One day, Harry Barber called in to see Will, looking very serious.

"He had to go and help with a grounded butty boat," Penny told him.

"Please tell him I will be back this evening to talk to him."

"Will you stop for a cup of tea?"

"No, thank you; mustn't stop. Too many urgent things to see to."

With that, he swung himself into his trap, flicked the pony, and set off at a cracking pace.

All morning, Penny wondered what was wrong. There was talk of their stretch of canal being taken over by one of the railway companies. If that happened, would they be able to stay? Was the job safe?

It was late when Will arrived home for his lunch. Penny let him eat it in peace, but when he made to put his boots on again, she told him of Harry's visit.

"Well, I can't say I'm surprised; I hear he has inherited his father's farm. Also, it seems we are to become part of the railway."

"But what about us? Will you still have your job?"

Will took her gently by the shoulders and said, "Don't fret before the event. Let's see what transpires."

After Will returned to work, Penny popped young Michael into his pram and set off to see Martha.

"Hello, this is a pleasant surprise." Stuart was just leaving the house as they arrived. "Martha is in the nursery with Peggy. I can't tell you how pleased I was to get that lass back. She is such a help to Martha and indeed to me, since you taught her to read. She does all the filing these days as well as making the appointments. We will miss her in the autumn. She has a place at St Thomas's."

"Oh, I'm so happy," Penny said. "She is such a kindly person; she'll make a wonderful nurse."

Penny forgot her own misgivings on hearing the news. Peggy Booth had become more than an employee, more like one of the family. They had helped one another while Will was away on the underground and in doing so had formed a firm friendship.

In the nursery, Penny found Martha and Peggy sorting out John's clothes.

"Do you know he has outgrown virtually everything?" Martha said proudly. "I believe he will be tall like Stuart."

Penny laughed. "You are so proud of that boy. And Peggy, congratulations."

"Oh, I wanted to tell you myself," she cried.

While the two little cousins played together, the two sisters and their friend started chatting about when they did their nurse training. They recalled old times and had a good laugh together.

Soon enough, it was time to meet Tim from school; they took their leave of one another, and Penny set off with a smile, worries put aside for the moment.

As she was putting the dishes away that evening, there was a tap on the front door, and she heard Harry Barber's voice as Will showed him into the front room. The two men were talking earnestly. After about an hour, Penny took them in some tea and biscuits.

"Dad had a good second income from supplying hay to the draught horses at the brewery," Harry was saying. "He employed a man to take the hay round to his customers. But now that Dad died, he wants to give up. Says he feels it needs a younger man. I shall have my hands full with the farm. I want to do more potatoes, cabbage, lettuce, and other cash crops to keep me going. So if you decide to take on haulage again, I should be able to put some work your way. I know I shall miss this life, but you may be lucky and be able to stay on."

There was no doubt that he had enjoyed working on the canals. But now duty was calling, and he had to return to the family farm.

Penny could see Will's excitement. He was off with his big ideas again. To move again so soon would be a blow, for the regular income had been a big bonus.

After Harry left, Will sat on in the room, deep in thought. It was possible he could stay with the canal. But it was going to be new employers and a new manager, anyway. So why not start on his own again now? The problem was that they live in a tied cottage; it was not just a wharf he wanted but a house as well. It was going to need a lot of thought, and he had just four weeks before Harry left to take on his father's farm.

"If you really want to start again," Penny told him, "you will need a strategy."

"How do you mean?"

"It's no good getting us another house and then finding a wharf miles away. Surely, as you are a current employee, you can tap into the grapevine and find out where there is a wharf available."

Penny was exasperated. This was the closest they had come to domestic discord. She was normally easy-going but felt it was arrogant of Will to make this kind of decision without listening to her point of view.

"It will be a big upheaval for all of us all," she said, "not least of all for Tim. He will have to settle into another school after only two years of this one. You must make sure we only move the once."

"I see your point," he said, relieved to find it was not that she didn't want to move on, simply that he had only been thinking about the business, not the domestic arrangements.

"Right, that's settled then. Would you like a cup of tea?" Penny had made her point. Getting a wharf was Will's responsibility; domestic arrangements fell to her, and she liked to be in charge and do things in an orderly manner.

CHAPTER 18

A Move up the Cut

B & B

Harry Barber's successor was a short, bumptious man with a braying laugh. He came from a large family who had worked the canals for years. Will was sure he would want the cottage for one of his relatives. He was at his wit's end. He had not been able to rent a wharf anywhere near a suitable accommodation for the family. Then there was the problem of stabling for the horses. Then quite suddenly, a wharf became vacant at Yiewsley Bridge. Adjacent to it was an old cottage, desperately in need of repair.

Will made an offer for the wharf subject to the old cottage being included, and to his surprise, it was accepted. Now he had to enlist the help of his family to make the home habitable. For as soon as it was in a reasonable shape, he intended to give his notice to the railway company. "Now we have a wharf and a house," Will said, sounding very excited, "we can set up as coal merchants as well as a hay carrier for Harry Barber."

But Penny sounded a word of caution: "It is getting late in the year. and we don't have a horse and cart or a stable."

"I'm thinking of getting one of those Model Ts with a flat body. Then I could get started with coal and haulage. Perhaps even run the local produce up to Borough Market."

That sounded like an excellent plan to Penny. That evening, they had an opportunity to talk it over with Martha and Stuart.

After the children went to bed, the four of them sat around the fire, the two men enjoying a pipe together. Will told Stuart he was thinking of getting a Model T.

"Good heavens! You are going to be stealing a march on the horse and cart. Did you hear that, Martha? Will is going to buy a Model T."

Martha smiled. "There you are, then. Will has beaten you to it. I tried to get you to buy one. Think how much quicker you could do the rounds."

The two men fell into conversation about speed ratios and combustion, which left Martha and Penny completely out of their depth.

"Let them get on with it," Martha said, shaking her head and laughing as she brought out new patterns for summer frocks. "I thought you might like to borrow these. Perhaps Peggy could do some of the smocking; she is very clever at it." Leaving the men to their discussions, they were soon engrossed in the latest fashions.

That afternoon, when it was time to go, Martha called to Penny, "Next time, we come, it will be by car."

Later, Will whistled softly to himself as he got his things together for the next day's work.

"I shall be back early tomorrow, love. Stuart and I are going to look at these Model Ts for ourselves."

"Does that mean it's definite?"

He laughed and said, "No, but probable."

Penny gave Will a hug; she was excited. The long wait was over. The adventure was about to begin.

CHAPTER 19

Black Gold Coal

ℬ ℐ ℬ

Will had found it hard work, sorting out the cottage. His father and brother Sam, home on leave from the Navy, did a great deal of the work. The new flat-bottom Model T lorry had proved its worth, carrying the building materials and cutting the cost by being able to buy in bulk and transport wood, tiles, cement, and other building materials.

By the time Will's one-month notice was up, the cottage was at least waterproof. The earth floors were replaced with concrete and a new stove installed; doors had been hung, glass put in the windows, and holes in the ceiling patched. Now all it needed was decorating. There wasn't enough time left for paper hanging, so they gave everywhere a quick whitewash, hung chintz curtains on wires at the windows, and were ready to move in.

The moving day dawned bright and dry, much to their relief, as everything was to be loaded on the lorry.

"Come on, Tim, hold on tight now." Will lifted Tim's dog up, and there they sat, boy and dog, in the middle of the load on a settee.

"Right, you're safe enough there." Will turned his attention to his wife and his younger son. "Do you think you could squash in together?"

Michael was already climbing into the cab. He was so excited; everything was so new to him. He would be starting school soon and had been looking forward to going with his older brother. Now he was sitting in the front of the new lorry while his older brother rode outside. So just for once, he was top dog. But the rivalry was soon forgotten when they pulled into the coal yard and saw the newly painted cottage.

Will's parents and brother were waiting to help them unload. The kettle on, they soon had the table and chairs unloaded. The picnic basket was found, hands washed under the pump in the yard, and they sat down in the new home to cold chicken pie and salad, which was just as well, as the boys were both famished.

Afterwards, they helped to unpack the tea chests with the crockery and pans for the kitchen, while the adults carried the furniture in and made up the beds for the night.

Tim enjoyed living right beside the canal. His friends now called for him by barge. He would hear the sound of the butty boat alongside the wall and then the sound of hobnails on the cobbled yard. Then pebbles would rattle on his bedroom window. He was greeted by the smiling face of Ginger Carson.

"You going to lay there like a rock all day?"

"Coming; just let me get my socks on."

"You want more than socks today. It is brass monkey weather."

After a hot cup of tea, the boys helped unload the boat. Tim held open the bag while Will shovelled coal in. His friend Ginger and his brothers helped fill the barrows, which were then walked precariously along a plank. When they had finished, they were as black as ink. Penny had the bath ready in the washroom with water from the copper. Will was first to dip, as he never seemed to get as dirty as Tim. By the time Ginger stepped into the water, it was very dirty indeed. But if he was going to school with Tim, he had to clean up quickly. His family lived on board a boat, and it was not often that Ginger got a chance to go to school. He was determined to be able to read, write, and count. His mother did her best to teach him. But in such a small living area with other children, it was difficult.

"You are lucky to live in a house where you can go into another room," he said. "It is really crowded on the boat."

Tim knew he was better off than Ginger. Even so, he longed to have the same freedom as his friend. Sailing all the way to the Midlands, his friend had a greater experience of life than he had. He longed to be a traveller.

The Model T certainly got the deliveries done quickly, but for running a weekly trolley service, nothing could compare to a good horse and cart. The horse got to know the route and would move on to the next house without having to be told, while the Model T had to be started and stopped, which used a lot of petrol. So it wasn't long before Dobbin and Star joined them.

Will built a stable in the yard, and the two horses were given a rest in turn at Harry Barber's farm.

At first, Will was very grateful for the contract to take hay supplies to London, as it took time to build a clientele for fuel. He often worried at the enormity of the risk he was taking. What if he should fail this time? But in his heart, he knew he wouldn't. For Will was a stubborn man, and for all his thirty-nine years of struggling, he had not lost the drive to get to the top of the pile. But despite his determination, he had never been blessed with any luck until now.

It was a bitterly cold winter, and many were without food or shelter. The country was in a state of unrest, and an awful depression built up. Unemployment grew, and anger mounted, so it was that strikes started. The railways came out on strike. Will was the only coal merchant with waterside loading (the barges were still sailing on the Grand Union Canal).

Overnight, he had become not only a retailer but a wholesaler to other coal merchants too. And those who had charged him full price for the odd bag when he was awaiting deliveries on his supplies in the past, he now charged full price on tons. And they paid. For they knew he would take their customers himself if not. Will had learnt to be hard in business, and success was his now.

The boys were growing fast, Tim now nearly as tall as his father, and Michael now at school. Penny was filled with pride to see them rising early and even the little lad polishing the horse brasses while his elder brother mucked out and groomed the horses.

At last, they had broken through the constant threat of poverty, but all around them, their neighbours had not. Little by little, Penny found some of their friends no longer quite as friendly.

"Take no notice," Will said. "They just envy us our good luck."

But Penny felt singled out and no longer one of them. Fortunately, Will's parents were quite close and were always pleased to see them. Penny often drove the children over to see them after school, and they often went with Will on Sunday; today was one of those days.

"How I wish you were still at Curlew cottage," Thomas mused. "It was great fun bringing all the produce to market and having the boy to take fishing." He ruffled Tim's hair. "When are you coming fishing with me again, eh?"

Tim flushed; he couldn't tell the old man that he was twelve coming on thirteen. Why, he was nearly a man now. He could hardly go fishing with his grandad. What would his friends say?

Instead, he muttered something about helping his father.

"Well, never mind, you're a good boy to help your dad," Thomas replied.

Tim felt his mother's eyes on him and felt very, small indeed, for he had noticed the tone of disappointment in the old man's voice.

For some time, Stuart had been so busy that he rarely had time to visit, but now he had a locum to look after his share of the practice, and he planned to take Martha and John for a visit to Sussex in the Model T.

"Come with us," Martha said. "You haven't had a holiday in years. No longer than a week anyway."

Penny wondered what Will would make of it.

But after she told him, he said, "You go and take the boys. I can manage here. It would do you good to have a change."

On the appointed day, they set off with Tim, Michael, and John in the back with Penny; it was a bit of a squash. Stuart was in fine fettle, with Martha in the front, and the suitcases were strapped to the side.

As they got nearer to Icklesham, the excitement rose. Even before they had pulled up, Lizzie was at the gate, with Bill not far behind, with Jane, Jason, and their son Peter, who was now as tall as Tim. He had filled out and lost the sickly look he had had as a young child.

"My word, Peter, you have grown in the fresh air," Lizzie said.

Jane also had lost her transparent look and gained a little colour in her cheeks.

"You have looked after them well, Jason," she added. "They are a credit to you."

Jason beamed and said, "Yes, I'm well pleased to have such a lovely wife and helpful son."

Lizzie showed them into the sitting room where tea and sandwiches were laid out ready.

"We can't sleep you all, but there are rooms ready for some of you at the Robin Hood. Just to sleep; we can all eat here."

The boys were soon off playing with their cousin and his friends.

"Now don't go far," Martha fussed. "We want to keep an eye on you."

"They'll be alright," her father said. "I have set up cricket for them in the field. We can sit in the garden and watch them play."

While the boys played, they had another cup of tea and chatted, catching up on the news. John Cooper was evidently now a very, successful farmer and, according to gossip, now a teetotaller. Penny found this hard to believe, but she was pleased to know he had prospered, after all. She had no regrets; she had found Will, and they were now comfortable.

Bill Thompson was busy talking politics with Stuart.

"It doesn't look good," Bill said. "A lot of trouble in the Balkans; shouldn't be surprised to see things hot up in Russia. They do say the Czar is very hard on his people. And the Czarina is famous for listening to that Rasputin, a wicked man if ever there was one."

"Well, I don't suppose it will make much difference to us here," Stuart replied. "Since Edward VII died, this king seems to be advocating family values. It ought to improve, although there is terrible poverty in the rural areas. People seem a little more settled."

"I wonder; beneath the surface, there is much discontent."

The two men fell into silence, each with his own thoughts; neither could have known how great the upheaval would be when at last the storm broke.

CHAPTER 20

A World Turned Upside Down

B & B

The demand for coal was not great during the warm summer. Will, Penny, and the boys stayed busy, helping out at Harry Barber's farm with the haymaking. Penny had packed a good picnic with plenty of drinks for the boys: dandelion and burdock, ginger beer, and lemonade. For the grown-ups, there was a barrel of cider. It was hot work but enjoyable, as all the locals had come to help, and the company was lively.

No one realised that this idyllic scene, a glorious day of blue skies, sunshine, shared tasks, and friendly banter was soon to be overshadowed by war. The horses shook their manes and flicked their tails to dislodge the flies, as unhooked from the wagon, they made their way home, the smallest of the children on their backs. It had been a long day, but now the hay was safely in. Tomorrow, Will and Harry would set about thatching the stacks. Already, the farmboys were collecting spliced hazel, and the thatching needles were laid out, ready to get an early start.

As Will and Penny set off for home with the boys, they heard a paperboy shouting, "Archduke shot, read all about it."

Will stopped and bought a paper and said, "Seems Archduke Ferdinand has been assassinated in Sarajevo."

"Oh dear," Penny said. "Will it mean trouble? Dad and Stuart were talking about the Balkans when we were on holiday. Dad seemed to think there was a lot of unrest beneath the surface, but I thought he meant here."

"Well," replied Will, "there is a lot of unrest, but it could be more general. I just don't know. Don't suppose it will affect us much."

They drove home, each thinking their own thoughts.

Shortly afterwards, like dominoes falling, Austria declared war on Serbia, and Germany declared war on Russia and then France, but they also marched into Belgium; this was too much for Great Britain, who declared war on both Germany and Austria-Hungary. Throughout that weekend, Penny and Will heard the unfamiliar rumble of trains through the night. The government had taken over the entire rail network, and for the duration of the war, the machinery of war took priority. Troops were being moved to the ports, reservists were being called up, and the railways were closely guarded. Mobilization of the regular army began on August 4. Sam, Will's brother, had been on manoeuvres in the Channel, but they did not come home, for at the end of the July, on Winston Churchill's orders, they proceeded to battle stations in the North Sea. It was the summer camp season. Many recruits were paid the King's shilling and immediately mobilised; some never went home.

Penny told Will she was pleased her sons were too young to go.

"Anyway, it will all be over by Christmas," he said. "The Kaiser won't want a serious rift with the Royal Family to go on for long. After all, he is Victoria's grandson, just as our king is."

But the war dragged on. Everywhere, posters appeared with Kitchener pointing his finger, saying, "Your country needs you." Thousands of farmworkers volunteered, but it was harvest time, which created havoc.

Will was in great demand, hauling in the crops with his horses and wagons. But he felt a growing unease. "I should be out there doing my bit for the country," he told Penny.

"Don't be so rash," she replied. "You have the coal business to run; how would people keep warm this winter without fuel?"

She certainly did not want Will to volunteer. But he continued to fret and, unbeknown to Penny, called in at the army office to enlist.

The squire from Iver was the enlisting officer. He looked surprised to see Will.

"What can I do for you, Long?" he asked.

"I wish to enlist, sir," he replied.

The squire looked at him long and hard. "I don't know about that. You do a very important job here at home. Who will keep the families supplied with fuel? No fuel, no cooking on the ranges. Families, cold and hungry. Don't suppose the boys at the front would be too pleased if they didn't think their families were being cared for. Be a good chap; just go home and get on with it."

Demoralised, Will turned and left. When he got home that night, he was quiet and dejected.

"What's up?" Penny asked, but he dare not say, for he knew she would give him a good tongue pie if she knew where he had been.

Some commodities were in short supply, and prices were rising dramatically. Penny would give Tim some money and get him to queue at the, butcher's. If the queue was very slow moving, she would then relieve him and carry on queuing herself. It was very wasteful of her time, and for women working in munitions, it was impossible.

Tales of spies abounded; it was said that the local munitions factory, rumoured to be owned by a man with German connections, produced shells that were useless. But the women who worked there naturally denied this. It was all part of rumour and counter-rumour.

Tim was now working with his father. At fourteen, he was strong enough to do the trolley service. Ginger had left the barge and enlisted as a boy soldier. Stuart enlisted in the Medical Corps, and Martha worried about him constantly. Old Dr Millard was rushed off his feet, delivering babies at regular intervals after home leave.

Nothing could compare with the bloodbath across the Channel. Village life was grim too. Many of the men were gone. None of them knew what they were volunteering for; many knew little of their own country, never mind France.

People began to criticise the financial policies of the government. Economise, they told people. Didn't they know that people had never done anything else? Invest in war bonds, they said; how?

"Why can't Prime Minister Asquith sacrifice a of tenth of his vast income (and, come to that, the rest of the government)?" the dissenters cried. But for the Long family, this was not a bad time financially. The coal business continued to prosper. Most farmers were also fairly well off, and many had arrangements with shopkeepers and so never went short. Many poor farmworkers volunteered just to get away from the grinding poverty and damp conditions they lived in. But the government encouraged patriotic women to work the land, and this helped the farmers no end, as they continued to pay low wages.

In the spring of 1915, the biggest threat to supplies was the submarine blockade. Fortunately, it eased in the summer, and adequate supplies of wheat came into the country from America and Argentina. It was distributed by canal, and Will and Tim were busy delivering it to shops and bakeries after it was milled. Offloading the bags of wheat for transport to the millers was really hard work. But they managed it with the help of a small crane and cradle. By contrast, deliveries to the bakers and shops were much more rewarding. Their two horses had been spared as essential workers. But most people had had their horses requisitioned to pull gun carriages and replace those lost by the cavalry. Tim was able to make deliveries using the cart, while Will drove the Model T to and from the mill.

News from the front was not good. Casualties were mounting, Stuart had not been heard of for some months. Everyone dreaded receiving a yellow telegram, a sign of bad news from the War Office.

Martha and John came to stay. One day, the telegraph boy arrived with the dreaded yellow envelope. Martha could not bring herself to open it.

"You open it, Penny," she cried.

Nervously, Penny opened it and read it out to Martha: "I have to inform you that Captain Stuart Wright has been wounded in action."

"Dear God," her sister said. "Thank goodness he is not dead. Does it say how badly he is hurt? My poor Stuart, what shall I do?"

Penny was glad that Martha was staying with them, as she was in such a nervous state.

"They will contact you again when Stuart has been evacuated to hospital," Penny explained. "Hang on to hope; he is alive."

Will was very quiet for days after hearing the news of his brother-in-law. The old feeling of guilt had returned.

I should have been there, he told himself. He decided to try volunteering again.

As winter approached, the weather was appalling. Frosts and heavy rain meant very little wheat was planted in the autumn, and the spring sowing was late because of the wet. The bad weather continued, culminating in a freak blizzard at the end of March. Roots were still in the ground, and much ploughing remained to be done.

On the front, the trenches were a mire of mud. It was a very depressing time. Spirits in the country were at an all-time low.

Penny and Martha spent a lot of time knitting gloves and scarves for the troops. They also took turns serving soup to the troops passing through the station on their way to the front or on their way from the front to hospitals around the country.

In June, Kitchener was drowned when the *Hampshire* was sunk.

"Hope it wasn't divine retribution for pointing his finger at all those poor boys," Martha remarked, but she immediately wished she had kept her thoughts to herself when she realised how many casualties there were; one of them might well be Will's brother Sam.

The Battle of the Somme began in July and dragged on for months. Everyone scanned the casualty list in the papers. It seemed that hardly a family was without loss. By November, British losses were 420,000. The flower of British youth was gone. Still the war raged on.

Stuart had been sent home to Harefield Hospital. A shell had exploded at the field station where he was patching up the wounded, and he was badly disfigured by shrapnel. The wounds to his body were nothing compared to the psychological damage he experienced. He suffered the most awful nightmares and was unable to return to his practice. Dr Miller, who had taken over after Stuart enlisted, arranged to sell half of the practice, as it was now obvious that the stricken veteran would never be the same again, and the doctor was desperately in need of help. Many wounded men were returning home, and the local medical men were having to take on this additional burden.

Martha just did not know how to help Stuart. Because it was so distressing for John, it was decided that he would stay with Penny and Will, sharing Tim's room. He needed the chance to quietly study, as he was hoping to enter medical school.

America had declared war on Germany; their troops now joined the others in France. At last, the tide was turning, and there were victories.

Hindenburg's lines were smashed on a ten-mile front. But the Kaiser hung on for a full year longer before fleeing to Holland.

Will, wondered, why the Dutch would give sanctuary to him. It was hard to understand.

Will was still bitter. When he tried again to join up, he had been sent home as a key worker. During that awful time when casualties were so high on the Somme, some woman in the street had presented him with a white feather, calling him a coward. He felt so humiliated. He wanted to do his duty. Stuart had, and look what a state he was in. Peter had upped his age and gone in; Jane and Jason received a yellow telegram and now mourned for their only son. Even his own parents worried, now that Sam and Tom were both reported missing. What had Will done?

Well, he been there to help families while their men were away. He had repaired roofs, transported people to hospitals to see their loved ones, and kept the home fires burning; he made sure the crops were harvested and grain was distributed, and he was a shoulder to cry on in troubled times.

"You do your bit right here," Penny told him. "The squire was right; you are needed more at home."

At last, an armistice was signed. For a while, the whole country seemed numbed by the terrible catastrophe that had befallen it (an awareness of just how many people from the colonies had fought alongside the British, and the terrible losses they had suffered in a European war, hundreds of miles from home). Things would never be the same again. New horizons had been shown to many, and their aspirations were now for a better standard of living than they ever dreamed of.

But times were still bleak. Young people adopted an attitude of jollity, in spite of a great deal of poverty. Saturday night became dance night. The Big Band sound was in. Youngsters danced the night away, doing the Black Bottom and the Charleston. Skirts became short, hats cloche shaped. Men wore boaters on their heads and Oxford bags for trousers. Music halls were all the rage. Will and Penny went up to Chiswick Empire on the tube train. You could hear delivery boys whistling the current songs from the shows.

Now nineteen, Tim enjoyed the dancing and partying. But Michael, who was considered old enough to work but not to dance and party with his older brother, had a new hobby: He was a pigeon fancier. He built himself a loft in the yard, and on Saturday afternoons, he trundled a cart loaded with baskets of the birds to the rail station, where they were put on a train to destinations far from home. Fanciers at the journey's end released the birds, who then flew home, racing against the clock. Many of the fanciers, who were all working men, laid bets on the winners. There were endless discussions in the pub that evening to discuss the finer points and drown any disappointment in a pint or two of beer.

Penny, meanwhile, had taken an interest in antiques. She now searched the junk shops and auction rooms for pot lids and Stevengraphs, Will was also bitten by the collecting bug. He now had an amazing collection of horse brasses and martingales. But the cottage was small, and it was not long before they were constrained by lack of space.

One day, Will had to collect hay from a new customer. He followed the directions, which took him to a farm that was formerly part of a gentleman's estate. The gatehouse at the entrance was in a state of disrepair. He continued down the drive, eventually turning off just before a mansion that lay in ruins. When he finally came to the farm, the farmer was out in the yard and showed him which barn the hay was in. He also instructed his boy to help with the loading.

"When you are finished, come up to the house for a drink before you leave," he said to Will. "We may be able to do more business together."

"Thank you," Will said, smiling. "I will do that." It was a kind gesture, as Will was hot and tired. He hoped the drink would be a nice cold beer.

"How long have you worked here?" Will ask the boy.

"Only since I left school last year. We moved here after Dad managed to buy this place."

"What, the whole estate?"

"No, only the home farm; the son was killed in the war, and when the old chap died, his wife lost heart and moved away. There is no family left now. My dad was at school with the son; they were great friends."

After they finished, Will called at the house and over a cup of tea learned more about the family who had been so cruelly wiped out by the war. The old squire's home had been gutted by fire after his son's death.

"Death duties crippled the estate. Two deaths in such a short time. So many of the workers never returned; the gatekeeper died at Ypres. His wife and children went back to her folks I believe." The farmer looked thoughtful as he remembered old times. "The squire's wife sold off parts of the estate. I was at school with Richard, her son; we were always friends. I bought the home farm and for the moment manage the remainder of the estate. So if you want more hay, the estate can provide it. There are no horses in the stables now."

Will listened to this tale and knew in his heart of hearts that life in the country, especially in the rural areas, had taken such a mortal blow that it would be generations before it recovered.

"I don't suppose the house will ever be rebuilt," the farmer said. "Lots of these big houses will come on the market now. No sons to run them, and in some parts, few workers for those estates that are left."

The man was obviously from the upper classes himself and sounded as if he regretted the passing of the old system. Will thanked him for the refreshments and set off for home. A thought had entered his head. Could he buy one of these large houses with an acre a two? After all, his family was comfortably off now, and he knew Penny would love a house with a walled garden. Just thinking of it made him smile.

CHAPTER 21

Love and Steam

B · B · B

The following summer, Will and the boys, made a lot of hay. Because so few workers were available, they were able to buy as much standing grass as they could. Harry Barber made storage available in his stack yards for a reasonable rent. He himself was now doing more market garden produce and making his farm pay. Those who stuck to traditional farming were now finding the going tough. Unemployment in the towns and cities was once again rising and prices for crops falling.

As people learnt that they could have fields mown and be paid for the grass, more farmers and estates contracted Will, and he did indeed see many estates falling into a state of disrepair. At this time, few ancestral homes were coming on the market. Farms were sold off by many estates, and probably more changed hands than ever before; the sitting tenants could struggle and buy their farms with a mortgage, but only by frugal living could they hang on; most homes and outbuildings needed maintenance and modernization.

Tim took most of the deliveries to London. Much of the hay was taken to large stables at the Elephant and Castle, where horses and carriages were looked after by ostlers. For the most part, these men were jolly cockneys and took a liking to Tim; some became good friends, in particular, a fellow called Jim Larkin. They often met up after work either for a drink or to go to the music hall.

Like many other ostlers, Jim slept at the stables, for the horses had to be made ready early in the morning. One day, having delivered his load, Tim went looking for his friend.

"Where is Jim Larkin?" he asked an old chap,who was chewing a plug of shag tobacco.

The man slowly removed the plug and spat in the corner before answering Tim.

"He's finished up and gone home," he said at length.

"Why would he do that?" He couldn't believe his friend should just clear off like that, without saying anything.

"Got a bad cough, he has; haven't you noticed it?"

He had noticed but thought it was just a bad cold hanging on.

"Do you know where I can find him?"

The old man thought for a moment.

"Comes from Bermondsey way, as far as I know," he replied.

Tim thanked him for his help and headed back home, determined to find his pal.

It took a lot of asking around to find where the Larkins lived. At last, he found the place in a dark alley off Wolsey Street, Farth Alley, it was called.

"Can you help me please?" he said, knocking on the door of a cottage. "I'm looking for Jim Larkin."

"Well, you've come to the right place," the woman answering the door said, "but he isn't here."

"Where can I find him?"

"In Switzerland."

"You're joking."

"No, he has gone to a sanatorium, along with his younger brothers; the Board of Guardians send the worst cases there. If the youngsters just look tubercular, they send them for spa treatment and solar rays."

"Do you have his address, please? He and I used to go for a drink or a show together."

"Well, come in," she replied. "I'm his mother, by the way."

Stepping in through the shabby door with chipped paint, Tim saw a small room, scrubbed tile floor, rug mats, several chairs, and a table. It was obvious that they were very poor; even the rag mats were much worn. But it was spotlessly clean. On the table was an unopened envelope.

"Now you are here," Mrs Larkin said, "perhaps you could read this for me. Jim always read things for me, but now there's only Alice and me, left here."

The door opened, and a young, very,beautiful woman entered.

"This is Alice," her mother said. "Alice, this young man is a friend of Jim's."

She smiled and quipped, "Aren't you a bit smart to be a friend of my bruvver?"

Tim felt his cheeks burn and said, "No, I'm not a bit smart. I just come from south-west."

"Where from in the south-west?"

"Iver, then we moved to Yewsley,by the canal."

"Don't keep questioning him," Mrs Larkin scolded. "Just make a cuppa; there's a good girl."

Alice disappeared into the scullery, and he could hear her getting the tea ready.

"Sit down and tell me about yourself, but first, would you read that letter?"

He picked up the envelope and opened it, glad to be able to look down at the paper and away from her amused gaze. The envelope bore a foreign stamp, and sure enough, it was from Jim.

"Dear Mum and Alice," he read. "George and Dick are making progress. The doctor says they will be as right as rain after two years. The food is good and the country beautiful. But I miss you both. I am still very tired, but I hope the fresh air and good food will see an improvement soon. Love to you both. Jim."

There were several crosses along the bottom of the page. Mrs Larkin was obviously moved. Her husband, a lighterman, had come to grief one foggy day when he slipped and fell between two boats. Times had been hard since then. The two young boys had worked whenever they could. But Jim had been their mainstay until he became sick. The doctor had been emphatic that to survive, he must have clean air. His brothers had caught the disease too and needed looking after. So, brooking no nonsense from any of them, he had sent them away. Partly because it was so contagious and partly because he was trying to save the young, who were often malnourished and living in such awful conditions.

Bermondsey had a Board of Guardians who were well ahead of their time, trying desperately hard to stamp out tuberculosis and address poverty. They paid relief monies above the national average, for many homes were without fathers.

When Alice returned with the tea, it was dreadful. Tim must have made a face because she looked him straight in the eye and said, "Leave it if you don't like it; it's sterilised milk."

"No, no," he protested. "It's just that I'm used to fresh, that's all." Then he asked her mother, "Do you mind if I copy Jim's address? Then I can write to him."

She nodded her agreement and asked, "Would you write one for me?"

Tim thought this a good idea: a readymade excuse to call and see Alice again.

"You tell me what to say, and I will see he gets it. For a start, I can write and say I've been to see you and how pleased you were to hear the news of the boys. And that you hope he soon feels chirpy himself. Then I will come and see you again next week. Perhaps Alice would like to send some messages?"

Alice was looking at him and smiling; he had the feeling that she knew what he was up to. There was a decided twinkle in her eye. He found himself blushing again and decided he better go.

"Until next week then," he said, picking up his cap.

"I'll see you out," Alice said.

That evening, Penny and Will heard him whistling as he took off his boots and hung up his coat and cap in the scullery. "Our Tim sounds happy," Will said. "Do you think he's in love?"

Over the next few months, it became obvious that this was the case. Whenever he had deliveries to the Elephant and Castle, he was late arriving home (and usually very happy too).

Eventually, Penny asked, "When are you going to bring her home?"

Tim had been dreading this. He was afraid that his parents might feel that Alice was not the right girl for him. He need not have worried, for the following Sunday, when he bought her home for dinner, both Penny and Will made her most welcome. Later that day, while Tim took her home, they sat around the fire, chatting.

"It's a pity she doesn't read and write," Will said. "That would be such a help to Tim and his business."

Penny laughed. "They haven't married yet; in any case, she could learn, like Peggy did."

"Yes, she did, thanks to you." He puffed on his pipe and gazed into the fire. "Funny thing is, she reminds me of Peggy. Lovely nature, that girl."

Michael had been so impressed by Alice that he told her, "Don't marry Tim; wait for me. I'll make you a good husband."

He was now apprenticed to be a carpenter. Always good with his hands, he had the making of a craftsman about him. He could not have been more different from Tim, who perhaps was more at home with horses and farm animals. He was an accomplished horseman, and Will often felt that beneath his western clothing, a Sitka brave was on the horse, erect and in control.

"You should tell him about his birth and the gypsy blood your mother's side," Penny said seriously. "Alice may not want him with a pedigree like that."

"Don't be silly; you didn't turn me down, did you?"

"No, but still, you had better tell him."

Will waited until an evening when he and Tim were sitting around the fire on their own. He didn't know quite where to start, but eventually, he outlined the story of being injured and nursed back to health by an Indian maiden. Throughout his story, Tim sat quietly. Will looked up to see what Tim's reaction was to the revelation of his birth, and to his surprise, his son seemed amused.

"Look, Dad," he said. "You don't have to make up a tale like that to cover your sins. You got Mum pregnant before you went to Canada to make your pile. She obviously forgave you for leaving her in the lurch. So why tell me this now? I think your story was quite a good one, though. Sitka Indian, indeed. Laughing to himself, he disappeared into the scullery to make a cup of tea.

Will sat there, dumbfounded; he hadn't even begun to tell him of his gypsy blood. Unless he wanted to be thought of as a great sprucer, it might be wise to say no more.

It was not long before they noticed a change in Tim. He seldom went out with the boys now and was more careful with his money.

"He is saving up to get wed," Will said one night. "Don't you agree, Penny?"

"Well, he has certainly changed. That girl is a good influence on him."

She really liked Alice, and having no daughter, she'd be pleased to have her join the family, but they seemed young to be thinking of taking on responsibilities.

Martha had written to say that she and Stuart were coming to see them all, but could they put up their parents as well? Lizzie and Bill hadn't been on holiday for years. Usually the family travelled to see them. Penny was excited.

"Pity you never found a stately home," she said to Will. "Life would be a lot easier if we had more room."

"I know, but I never found one without too many acres of land and a price to match. Besides, there would be no holding you back with your garden parties and croquet on the lawn."

Penny threw the duster at him and said, "Come on, then, help me move the beds. I'll just have to manage as we are."

Stuart had been staying at a convalescent home on the Isle of Wight. He looked fitter, although still bore the war's scars. But the tranquillity, fresh air, and quiet living had helped to settle his nerves. Martha was very protective of him, and he obviously leaned heavily on her. He would never return to his profession. Jason had been showing him how to market garden. They were now hoping to extend the acreage to enable him to work permanently with Jason. With access to more vegetables, they would be able to supply not just greengrocers but hotels and boarding houses in Hastings and Bexhill. It would mean having another horse and cart or maybe a Model T Ford lorry. Stuart had the capital and Jason the local knowledge and growing experience. Lizzie and Bill were delighted with this plan. They never dreamed when they set up their market garden that it would eventually support two of their daughters and their families. Although Stuart had a very traumatic time, he seemed to accept a quieter way of living. For Jane and Jason, the extension at the market garden gave them a new impetus to life. Losing their only child could so easily have destroyed their lives.

Will went to the station to collect the in-laws. He brought them back home, and they chatted over a cup of tea.

"Jason and Jane are holding the fort while you are gadding about on holiday, eh, Stuart?"

Stuart laughed good naturedly at the teasing.

"I hope to find a lorry suitable for deliveries to hotels and boarding houses," he replied. "You could say I am doing research."

"You'll probably want one with canvas to keep the fruit and veg dry. Foden's are doing some very good delivery vehicles, unless you want to go for a Ford again."

"Listen to them," Martha said. "It's just like old times. They'll be talking about gear ratios any minute."

"Well, one thing to be said for a lorry," her mother replied. "You don't have to groom it, feed it, and muck it out."

"Best to have both," Bill said. "But I don't suppose I should drive."

"Why not, Dad? You'd enjoy it." Will was teasing again. "Tomorrow, I will let you deliver the coal, get your experience here."

"No, Will. I'm too long in the tooth to start learning a whole new way."

"Stop your teasing now, Will. Dinner is ready."

Still laughing and ribbing one another, they made their way to the dining room. The family sat around the table with a bottle of wine to celebrate; Will proposed a toast to those who were not present: John away at his medical studies, Jason and Jane minding the market garden, and Peter, the boy who had shown so much promise. Penny felt so lucky to have her family around. You never know what life might fling at you. For her, it had been fortunate. For Martha and Jane, the war had been a disaster. She wondered just how much her parents were still grieving. After all, Peter had been the only grandchild they had seen grow up in every stage of his young life.

Will took Stuart to see how fruit and veg were distributed at Borough Market and Covent Garden. Then they went to see new models of delivery vans. Eventually, they came across a Foden van, complete with a flat bottom for easy loading and canvases to protect the produce from sun and wet weather. Stuart bought it and arranged for Will to drive it back to Icklesham. The rest of the party followed by train.

"You go with them," Tim told his parents; he was certain he could run the business while they were away. "Michael will help with the horses, won't you?"

"Of course, I will. And I can do the trolley deliveries, but who will cook our meals?"

Tim blushed slightly and replied, "Alice can stay with my friends and come over to get dinner."

"That's it, boy. Find out if she's a good cook before you tie the knot," his grandfather said.

"Really, Dad," Penny snapped. "What a thing to say." She did not think Alice would like to hear these comments about her capabilities.

"Is it serious, then?" Will asked his son.

"Oh, yes. I have asked her if she was prepared to take on a Sitka brave, and she said, 'Yes, provided I don't live in a tepee.'"

Everyone laughed and then congratulated him. As Tim thought it a huge joke. Will decided to let it be. Perhaps it was better to keep some things to yourself, he decided. After all, Penny had never told him what happened to her while he was in Canada. He guessed she had a past. But would he have been any happier if he knew the details? He thought not. The young ones were in love. Why spoil it for history's sake?

After a few days of sightseeing and socialising, Penny with her parents, and Martha travelled back to Hastings on the train, while Stuart and Will took the Foden by road to Icklesham. It took them longer than they expected, as neither had experience refuelling a steam engine, which required regular attention to maintain a good head of steam. They finally made it, hands and faces black as ink and big smiles on their faces. They had finally got it right and were very pleased with themselves.

After they arrived at home, Jason was as excited as they were and had to be taken for a ride before they had a meal.

"Come on, boys. Stop playing and let's have our meal," Lizzy called to them. But it was some time before they had washed up and sat at table. The conversation was of pounds of steam pressure and gear ratios.

"Here we go again," said Martha. "Same old thing. All hot air."

"Don't forget the gear ratios."

"Men."

Lizzy could wait no longer; she started to dish up the meal.

CHAPTER 22

The FA Cup at Wembley and the Empire Exhibition

☙ ❧ ☙

Tim went to the FA Cup final, the first to be held in the new Wembley Stadium. It had been built on a site proposed for the Empire Exhibition. He was fascinated by the buildings going up. The Palace of Engineering was said to be six and a half times the size of Trafalgar Square and the largest concrete construction in the world. There was a replica of the Taj Mahal and the Queen's dollhouse. A complete mansion was built on the scale of one inch to the foot.

The match itself was a terrifying experience. He had thought he was about to be crushed; three hundred thousand people were trying to get into a stadium built to hold 125,000. Eventually, two hundred thousand were inside the gates. When the Bolton Wanderers beat West Ham 2-0, the crowd surged again. This caused more casualties, but the heroism of one police officer, who starting at the centre had used his white horse to clear the pitch enough for the game to be played, saved the day. Even so, more than a thousand spectators were treated for injuries.

It took Tim hours to extract himself from the crowd. Shaken and excited, he made his way home. "Whew," he told his brother. "That was a close thing, but I wouldn't have missed the match for anything."

A year later, the Empire exhibition opened.

"We must see it," Tim told Alice. "It will be the greatest show in the world. See here, every country that is marked pink belongs to us."

He excitedly spread out a large atlas on the kitchen table. "They are all displaying replicas of their colony."

"I don't feel as if I own any of it," Alice replied. "But I would love to see the pageant. They say it has a cast of fifteen thousand. It is supposed to show the history of the British Empire."

Tim grinned and said, "They will tamper with the truth, then; can't see them admitting to employing slaves or selling opium to the Chinese."

"No, but a lot of people have helped," she replied.

"Or helped themselves to land, diamonds, and spoils of war."

"I still think the British are the best and winning the Empire a great feat. What about the missionaries? They have helped with education and orphanages as well as spreading the Word."

"But what about those families who made a fortune by exploiting slaves on the sugar plantations? Still, we should be proud of the Empire, if only as a very successful business venture."

Alice laughed. "Why do you always come back to that point, Tim? Business. Why do you have to work in your dad's business? He holds the purse strings."

"Don't talk like that. I'll talk to him and see if he'll give me a regular salary. We'll sort it out."

Alice did not look convinced.

"Look, I know he means well, but how can we get married and pay rent if we don't know we have the cash to pay our way?"

"It has never been a problem. When I wanted money to go out, he would just give me some."

"My mum said I should get it straightened out before we wed. Too late after, she says. I don't want to be having to ask for every shilling I spend."

"I promise it won't be like that, you'll see," he said; seeing that she looked worried, he put his arm around her and kissed her gently. "Forget it now. Let's have a look at this official guide to the exhibition."

They shelved any misgivings they had about their future and studied the guide. There were some lovely illustrations of the pavilion, lots of adverts, a map of the exhibition and the amusement park, together with numerous pictures of the Royal Family at the preview.

"It would be better to go in July or August," Tim said. "That's when the pageant is on. There is a rodeo with cowboys too."

"It does sound exciting. But we shan't be able to do it in a day. There are 220 acres."

Alice was staying for the weekend with Tim and his family. Penny and Will had been out to visit their friends, giving the young couple a chance to be alone. Now as they came in, they caught the end of the conversation.

"Two hundred acres?" Will exclaimed. "Where?"

"At the Empire Exhibition, Dad," laughed Tim.

"Shall we all go to it?" Will asked. "My treat. If we all go, we could hire a car. But I don't think we should try to do too much in one go. It is open all year, so we could go several times."

Everyone had ideas about what they would most like to see, and they decided to go the following Saturday. When they arrived, there were many people queuing. Will had purchased tickets in advance, so they were soon inside, leaving long queues waiting to pay their one shilling and sixpence to get in.

The two men spent a lot of time looking at the engineering, while Penny and Alice viewed the doll's house.

"That's the sort of mansion to have," Penny said. "Just look at how beautiful it is furnished."

"Tim said you're looking for a big house. Would you really like to live like the aristocrats?"

Penny laughed. "It really was a joke. I can't believe it will ever happen, but I would love to have a beautiful garden and more space."

"Imagine just ringing the bell and someone rushing to carry out your every whim."

"Steady on, Alice; don't let your imagination run off with you." Penny laughed again. "No one is going to rush to carry anything; it will be Joe Muggins who prepares tea."

"No, it won't." Will had heard the conversation as he came to join them. "We are dining out today."

There were plenty of places to eat; they chose a café with open-air seating, where they could watch the amusements. On offer, salad served with large Dublin Bay prawns.

"Cor," exclaimed Alice. "Just look at the size of those shrimps."

"I am having a knickerbocker glory for after."

"You'll never get that lot down you, Tim."

"You see if I don't," he replied.

After lunch, they went for a walk to see the sights. There were some military bands parading, dressed in smart uniforms of other lands. Alice was amazed to see the drum major turning his baton and throw it skywards, catching it before it would fell.

"I wonder how many times he had to practice before he could do it in public," she said.

This made them all smile.

"I want to know," Tim said, "how they put up with that billy goat in the barracks."

"Well, the goat keeper would have to bathe it daily, maybe twice a day."

Will was absolutely fascinated. "Just look at the Sudanese troops on camels," he said. "Now that's a nasty animal to care for."

It certainly seemed that he was right, for as they passed, they could hear snorting and growling.

Most of the troops wore turbans, and some men had on what could only be described as skirts.

Moving away from the tableaux, there were rides on an elephant, train rides around the show, tumblers from Hong Kong making amazing human pyramids, clowns amazing children, buskers, and an amazing array of pearly kings and queens from nearby London.

There was such a mix of cultures and gaily dressed people, with such a feeling of comradeship and pride. Every land showed what they contributed to the Empire. A huge body of smiling happy people joined in this huge celebration.

"What a wonderful showcase for the Empire," Will said. "There will never be such a spectacle to match this ever again."

Penny and Alice were giving their legs a much-needed rest, sitting on a seat facing the India pavilion across the lake. It was a peaceful scene depicting the Taj Mahal.

"It says that it was built by the maharaja as a tribute to his favourite wife, who he loved deeply," Penny read out.

"It is certainly beautiful. But I wonder if he told her how much he loved her. If not, it wouldn't matter to her that he erected this monument, would it?"

Penny was aware that Alice was questioning something in her own life.

"Alice, is there something wrong between you and Tim? Anything I can help with?"

Alice felt that she was being disloyal to Tim. She looked around to see if Tim and his dad were returning from the beer tent.

"Well, only that Tim wants to get married soon. But me mum says be sure he can support me and the family we have. How can I be sure when his dad only gives him pocket money? I don't want to be poor all my life."

Penny was shocked. "How could you think you'd be poor? We would always see that you had what you needed."

"But you don't understand. I want to manage my own housekeeping, not to have to ask for every last shilling."

"But when you are in business, things are seasonal. Sometimes, there is cash; other times, it can be tight. We couldn't guarantee a regular sum all year."

"I see," Alice replied glumly.

Tim and his dad returned from the beer tent, bringing ginger beers for Penny and Alice.

Realising that Alice was quiet, Tim squeezed her hand. "Pecker up," he said. "I've got it all in hand."

But Alice remained quiet. She feared she was just going to be absorbed into Tim's family. But she wanted them to have the freedom to make their own decisions. Tim wasn't, a bit worried about their future. His dad was generous when he had cash, and Tim got into the habit of saving half or more each time he was handed any money. He now had quite a bit laid by, but he hadn't told Alice. He was already building his own business empire in his mind. He planned to build workshops and lease them to people to start their own light engineering businesses or motor repairs. He just needed to find the right piece of land at the right price. Already development was taking place along the Great West Road. Gillette had built a place there, as had Firestone tyres and Bovril, displaying their advert, "Don't get tired; drink Bovril."

Thousands of Welsh miners had come south, displaced from the mines, and it was to this area around London that they had come seeking work in the many new industries that were opening up.

Tim hadn't intended to get married so young. Meeting Alice had upset his plans. But he was already thinking ahead. When the exhibition was over, there would be land available, already served by roads and public services; he aimed to buy some of it. This was his dilemma. Should he tell Alice and risk upsetting her? She might feel he should spend his capital on their home. Or should he wait until he had secured the land? There was also the problem of telling his father he was thinking of branching out on his own. His dad would be sure to want to come in as a partner, but he wanted to go it alone. Thinking it over, he decided to keep it to himself, at least for the time being.

Tim recently heard from his old pal Jim, who had written to say he understood he was soon to be his brother-in-law.

"You artful old sod," he had written. "Pinchin' my lovely sister while I am cooped up over here. George and Dick will be discharged in two or three months, but yours truly will have to soldier on until the end of the year; even then, they are advising a life in the open air. If you have any suggestions what I might turn my hand to, I will be glad. Cheerio for now, Jim."

Tim was delighted to hear from Jim, especially as he sounded so positive. He knew Alice and her mother worried a great deal about them, and now the two youngest were returning, and Jim would be back soon. Tim really missed his friend and couldn't wait to go over to Alice's home to tell her the good news.

Mrs Larkin was delighted. "We must move from here," she said. "I can't have those two boys coming back here with the bad air. I must get them out into the country."

"What could they do?" Alice asked. "They don't need lighterman in the country."

"Hang on a minute, Alice," Tim interrupted. "They could become bargees, and come to think of it, Jim could get a job with the hunt or maybe become a gamekeeper."

"Gamekeeper would be a good job for Jim. They do seem to have a good life if they can get on a well-run estate." Mrs Larkin was evidently pleased with Tim's suggestion. "Would you be able to ask around when you're delivering the hay?" she asked.

"I will listen out for word for any vacancies on the Cut. I'm sure to hear something. I get to talk to quite a lot of bargees when they deliver to our wharf."

"That's settled then. Now, Alice and I must concentrate on getting a house nearer to the countryside, where we can still get work."

It wasn't easy, with so many people coming south; jobs were becoming difficult to find.

"We need to widen our circle," Alice suggested. "Perhaps we should look in the countryside rather than on the edge of towns; if there was a bus service, we could travel into work." She was studying the local paper. "There are some places available at Pinner, Ruislip, Eastcote, Hayes, Sipson, and Ickenham."

Tim asked, "Where do you want to start looking, then?"

"Ruislip," she replied.

Tim borrowed the lorry from his father, and with Alice sandwiched between him and his mother, they set off.

The cottage at Ruislip had that dank smell of damp that old houses sometimes have. The garden was small and overgrown. The little house, in a row with three other equally neglected cottages, was filthy. That was number one crossed off the list.

"How can people live like that?" Mrs Larkin exclaimed, as she climbed back into the lorry.

"Where to now?" Tim started the engine. "Can't be out too long. Mum and Dad are out today, and I promised to feed the horses."

"Right, so which is on the way home for you?"

"Well, Sipson if we go the long way round; shall we try Sipson today?"

Tim gave Alice a little smile, and she thought to herself, *Cheeky monkey; that is the nearest to his home.*

But like the Ruislip cottage, it was in a near derelict condition. Mrs Larkin had become very quiet. She looked tired and disappointed.

"Don't worry," Tim said to her. "We shall find you something in decent shape if we keep looking. If you don't mind waiting, I'll do the horses and then run you both, home."

Alice, grateful for his kindness to her and her mother, gently squeezed his hand.

Her mother, feeling something of a gooseberry, exclaimed, "Stop that hanky-panky; let's get home," which set both Tim and Alice off with giggles.

"I only held his hand, Mother," Alice said, laughing.

Still amused, they set off for Tim's home to feed the horses.

"Next weekend, we'll have better luck," Tim said. "You'll see."

He was feeling more optimistic as he sat in Mrs Larkin's kitchen having a piece of her homemade fruit cake and welcomed cup of tea.

"I only hope you're right because we have to get jobs as well before the boys come home."

Tim decided he would look at other potential properties before taking Alice and her mother to see them. That way, he could take some of the disappointment out of the search. But after a week of looking at everything available, he too was getting despondent.

He had seen a cottage in the village of Ickenham, and on the face of it, it had potential, but the roof was in very poor shape. The lady who showed it to him was leaving to live with her daughter, who needed to supplement her war widow pension, but as she had several children, her mother was going to keep the home for her.

"My mother left me this house. I shan't ask much, because as you see I haven't managed to keep it in repair. But you're a young man; you could put it right."

"Would you sell it to me if you don't think you'll be coming back?"

"I need the money. But you must make me an offer I can't refuse," she said with a smile.

Tim was doing a bit of calculation. He wanted to leave himself enough cash for his business, but he was sure he could fix this roof himself.

"Name the price," he said.

"Could you see yourself able to give me a hundred pounds?"

"Yes, agreed. But can you set an early date so I can get the roof done before the bad weather sets in?"

Tim rode home that night in a daze. He had bought a home, and he liked that feeling.

"Guess what?" he asked his mother. "I am a man of property."

"Yes," she replied, "and I am a lady in waiting. Waiting for you to sit down to dinner."

"No, Mum. I'm serious. I just bought a cottage."

"Well, you are a bit young, but Alice is a lovely girl."

"No, you've got it all wrong. I bought it for her and her mum. It needs the roof doing. I thought I could put a new thatch on myself. Alice's mum wants to get settled in a new job before the boys come home. We've looked at no end of places to rent, but they were all very run down. But this one I liked. They haven't seen it yet. But I'm sure they will like it when I smarten it up a bit. The lady who owns it is going to live with her daughter to help out. The daughter is a war widow with children, so she needs to work. I thought if I were to charge Mrs Larkin a small rent, I could save it up to give to Alice to buy her trousseau."

"It's a good idea, but you're getting ahead of yourself. Talk it over with her mother first. She may not even like the cottage. What will you do then?"

"Well, then it will be the first property in my portfolio. Remember, I aim to be a man of property."

CHAPTER 23

A Man of Property

ß ℰ ß

Tim was worried. Was his mother, right? Had he gone ahead too fast? But no, he had taken the opportunity when it was there. Had he waited the cottage might have been let before he made up his mind. But he knew Mrs Larkin was a very independent person. She might not like to be beholden to him. In the end, he waited to talk it over with Alice.

"Mum's going to think you bought it for us."

"But you can tell her you wouldn't leave her until the boys are home and settled. I don't want to rush things. I haven't,sorted it out with the old man yet. Financially, I mean."

"I know; let's not worry about that now. Take me to see the cottage, and then perhaps I can persuade her. Can you really put a new roof on yourself?"

"I hope so, I have thatched a few stacks, so I've got some experience."

On Sunday afternoon, Tim picked Alice up in the lorry, and they drove to Ickenham to see the cottage.

"Mum was a bit disappointed when you didn't ask her to come viewing properties," Alice said on the way.

"I know. I could see that she was ready to come. But I couldn't face her look of disappointment again. When we get there, try to imagine what it will look like with a new thatch and a lick of paint."

"Could I help with the painting?"

"Would you? I'd be glad of any help I can get. Here we are, just coming into view now."

Alice was entranced with the cottage and, in particular, the garden.

"Do you think your mum will like it then?"

"Like it? I'll say she will. We've never had a garden. Nor so much space in the house. It's got two big bedrooms and one small one. I shall have the small one for myself."

Silently, Tim was relieved he had not only bought a property, he had also bought time, time that he hoped to turn into a business opportunity.

"Shall we tell your mother now, or wait until I have done the roof?"

"Let's tell her now. I'm so excited."

So th.ey set off back to Alice's home.

When they arrived, Mrs Larkin was very quiet. She was obviously hurt, thinking they had abandoned the search for a property and just went out for the afternoon. But there was such an air of excitement about the young couple that she eventually asked them if they had been somewhere nice.

"Oh, very," Alice replied. "We viewed a lovely garden."

"It must be wonderful to have a garden to grow flowers and fresh vegetables," her mother said, sighing. "To be able to sit out in the sunshine must be a real treat."

"We'll take you to see it next Sunday. You'd enjoy that."

"I know, but I really should be looking for somewhere to live."

"Well, just this once, have a day off and come with us."

"You're very kind," she replied. "Now I must go and prepare tea."

"I'll come and help you, Mum." Alice smiled at Tim and gave him a big wink. What a relief. It looked as if all was well.

Tim and his dad were having a cold meat and pickle supper. They were doing a haulage job tomorrow, and an early start meant there was no chance to have a good breakfast. The goods had to be collected from the railway sidings and delivered to Mr Harding a farmer some twenty miles away.

"What is this load?" Tim asked. "Did he say?"

"I believe it is Welsh roofing slates. It seems they wanted enough to do the farmhouse, but it's cheaper to buy direct from the quarry and take a full load. You want to do a deal there, lad. Make them an offer for any surplus slates. Make a better roof than thatch for your cottage.

"Would they be difficult to fix?"

"No, they come with the small holes already in, and you just hang them and nail them to a batten. You would need to get some coping for the ridge, though. They could be pricey."

Tim went to bed thinking this suggestion over. True, it would make a better roof. But it was probably going to cost quite a lot more. He wasn't going to have time to price the copings before he made an offer for the slates, and he was going to have to deliver the slates to the cottage straight from the siding so he could get the steam crane to lift the crate onto the lorry. He would have to unpack the crates if he didn't want to get a hernia. To cap it all, he didn't know how many slates it needed. The only thing he could do was buy all the ones the farmer didn't need. With his head in a whirl, he dropped off into a troubled sleep. His demons kept him tossing and turning. In no time at all, it seemed, it was time to be up and off.

Will was already down in the kitchen, making a cup of tea. On the table were two packed lunches, a bottle of beer, and a stoneware bottle of ginger beer.

"It could be a heavy day's work," Will said. "But the farmer has promised to have a horse and flat cart to offload onto. I'll have a word with him and see what we can do about your slates."

This was exactly why Tim was so anxious to be in business on his own. He wanted to make his own decisions, not always be in his dad's shadow. But in this case, he had to admit to himself, he was all at sea. He didn't know what to offer or how many slates he'd need. So, he nodded his head in agreement and decided to let the day take its course.

The crates were unwieldy things, even with the help of the crane. By the time they had the first load on, both, of them, had knocked their knuckles.

"Are you sure this is a good idea, Dad?"

Will laughed and said, "Don't be faint-hearted; true love never runs smoothly, and your mother-in-law is going to think you're the bee's knees."

The horse and cart were there to offload the slates on to, and a couple of big strong farmhands to do it too.

Will went off to see the farmer, who was only too pleased to sell the surplus slates at cost, knowing that it was saving him a lot on carriage charges. He had also bought a whole load of copings.

"When you get that far with your roof," the farmer said, "come and see me. You'll know how many you want; better still, come and help with this roof, and in return, you can have your slates and copings."

"Well, I have to confess I haven't done a roof yet."

"Nothing to it; I'll show you how."

"Well, what do you think about that?" Will said, looking very, pleased with himself. "You'll be able to save yourself a few bob."

"Dad, have you seen the size of the farmhouse roof? Your ideas are alright up to a point. How am I going to fix that roof on my own before the weather breaks? Just tell me that, and there is still the hay to deliver and the coal. There just aren't enough hours in the day."

"You delegate; that's what I do."

"And don't I know it; I'm the poor devil running around like a bluebottle, trying to tie up all the loose ends."

"Don't get sore now. I was only trying to help. But why don't you get Michael to help you? It would be good experience for him. Get his hand in with a bit of general building work as well as the carpentry."

"He might see that as exploitation."

"Not if you pay him. Now you haven't got to buy your materials, you could employ him in the evenings and weekends."

"Now that is a good idea."

"I have them sometimes, I must admit."

Tim wondered how he was so sure of himself. Well, his dad always seemed to think big. Perhaps he was too cautious. It certainly seemed to work for Dad. He appeared fearless and never in awe of his so-called betters.

Now he had another hurdle to overcome. It was nearly the weekend again. He had to honour his promise to take Mrs Larkin and Alice out. This Sunday, he would know what Mrs Larkin thought of the cottage.

Alice was so excited; she had been up since dawn. Every now and then, she'd lift the net curtains and peer out to see if she could see Tim.

"Do sit down and relax," her mother said. "You're making me feel nervous. Better still, how about putting the kettle on? Perhaps we should have our breakfast too. Then we'll be ready when Tim arrives."

Alice disappeared into the small scullery and could be heard rattling the cups.

Mrs Larkin sighed and sat down wearily. If only she could get something sorted out for her boys. She was feeling exhausted and anxious. A week had gone by and still nothing.

She was startled from her thoughts by someone whistling a merry tune and the sound of nails on the cobbles. There was a banging on the door, and Alice called, "He's here. It's Tim."

"Your chariot awaits you at the end of the alley," he said. "I couldn't get down here this morning. Cart in the way. Someone doing a flit. Tim was looking very smart; polished shoes, creases in his trousers, and grease on his hair, stuck up at the back.

"Your very cheerful this morning, Tim," Mrs Larkin replied.

"Who wouldn't be, with such charming companions?"

"Why do I get the feeling you're trying to butter me up, young man?"

"Whatever gave you that idea?" He winked at Alice, who was enjoying every minute of this situation.

Still in good spirits, they left the house, carrying a basket of food and drink that had been prepared last night.

Tim helped Mrs Larkin up into the cab of the lorry and passed her the basket, which she insisted must be kept upright on her lap.

"It will be very heavy," he said. "Why don't you put it on the floor?"

"Because there's a special treat in there that I don't want spoiled," she replied.

They set off very carefully. The sun was shining as they edged their way out into the traffic. As they left the city behind them, they travelled in companionable silence, each with their own thoughts.

When at last they stopped outside the cottage, Tim knew that he need not worry if Alice's mother liked it.

"What a pretty cottage," she exclaimed, "and just look at those flowers. Alice, do you see those butterflies?"

Tim got down, opened the door for the two ladies, and helped them out of the lorry. Then with a flourish, he flung the gate wide and said, "Welcome to your new home."

Overcome with emotion, his future mother-in-law grabbed him in a bear hug and gave him a kiss on his cheek.

"I think she approves, don't you?" Alice said, laughing.

"Shall we look over it before we eat?" Tim asked. By way of an answer, the two ladies were already making for the door.

They were soon discussing what paper and paint they wanted and seemed quite disappointed when Tim suggested they wait until he fixed the roof.

Alice spread a rug out in the sun, and they ate their picnic, finishing with the special treat: a cream trifle and a drink of homemade lemonade. In the mellow early autumn sunshine, bumblebees and butterflies flitted to and fro; even a cricket still clicked away happily.

"What a wonderful day," Mrs Larkin said. "Thank you both so much. Such a surprise and the answer to my prayers."

That evening, they discussed what to take and what to leave. Tim had seen a tiny bedroom set, a wardrobe and dressing table, which he determined to buy for Alice. It was painted green with lovely red roses on the front of the drawers and doors. But he didn't tell her about the surprise.

Penny and Will were waiting to hear how things had gone at the cottage.

"Did Alice's mum like it?" Penny asked. She heard how Tim had been hugged and kissed. "You're flavour of the month, then. Just don't blot your copybook."

Michael, who had been reading in the front parlour, came in.

"I hear you are in need of a reliable roofer. Is the pay good?"

"Name your price. Seriously, I have taken on too much and desperately need help."

"We have rallied the family. Martha and Stuart are coming up with Jane and Jason. If Alice and her mother come over today as well, it will be a huge work party."

Tim, amazed, said, "What a wonderful family I've got."

"It's the only way we can show we care," his dad replied gruffly.

Each day, Tim and Will took a load of slates from the sidings to the farm until the farmer thought he had enough to do the roof. Meanwhile, Tim got as far ahead with his deliveries of coal as he could.

Alice and Penny did their best to sort out sleeping arrangements. When that was done, they turned their attention to cooking for the army of helpers. Alice's mother had been very busy cooking.

"Goodness, what a lot of lovely smells." Will had come into the kitchen to talk to Penny. "How about if I fetch my mum and dad over? They haven't seen your parents for years. It would be nice for the old folks to get together."

"What a lovely idea. It would be difficult sleeping them, though."

"Don't worry about that. I'll just run them home later. They'd like their own bed, anyway."

Will, who recently bought himself a smart new car, set off for his parents' house. Humming to himself as he drove along, he decided to go down memory lane, turning off the road and onto the path that took him past Curlew cottage. It was looking pretty as a picture. He remembered the struggle he had to survive there. But he also recalled the happiness with his family and the lovely times they had with Stuart and Martha. The war changed all that. So many other people he had known were lost. He was so lucky in his life, blessed with good health and his family around him.

Bill and Eliza were surprised to see Will in the daytime.

"Not working today, then?" his dad inquired.

"No," he replied. "I've come to take you back with me to see Penny's folks. They'll be arriving shortly. They've come to help Tim get the roofing jobs done before the bad weather sets in."

"Yes, he was telling us about the cottage," Bill said. "Thought perhaps he wanted it himself, though he is a bit too young to wed yet."

"He isn't quite ready; got some idea that he has to prove himself in business first." Will took a deep draw on his pipe. "I've been thinking of offering him a partnership. But if he could do something on his own, it might give him more satisfaction. What do you think?"

"He is bound to spread his wings sometime. I think I would play a waiting game. See what he does. You know what they say about not having two roosters in the same yard."

Will laughed. "So you reckon I'm a cocky bloke then, Dad?"

"Yes, I do. But it hasn't done you any harm; you've done well, son."

"Come on, you two; let's be off." Eliza stood in her finery, wearing her best go-to-church hat.

"My word, you look posh; this isn't tea with the Royals, you know."

"Well, you can go looking like a scruff, but I don't have to."

"Watch it, Dad; you're treading on dangerous ground."

The old man laughed and said, "She has always been sparky."

As they pulled into the yard, they could see the others had already arrived, and the noise of chatter and teacups came floating out the window.

"Hello, everyone," they called out as they went in.

They were soon joining in the general social event. Will noticed how well his parents and Penny's were getting on. Across the room, he could see Penny laughing at some joke of Stuart's. She looked so happy; he wondered just how much she missed her family. It wasn't often they were able to get together and never all at once, as they were now.

But this was a special occasion. They had all dropped everything to come and help his son. What kindness, it made him feel quite humble. A new experience for Will, who for a long time have been focused on getting on. Money had been his goal. He had made it, but it was perhaps time to be a little more generous. Acting as host, he circulated among his guests and filled up their glasses.

"You know, Penny," Martha said, "Will has certainly grown in confidence since you first brought him to dinner all those years ago. He had such squeaky shoes, and he was so nervous."

Tim overheard Martha's comments and said, "I don't believe it,my dad, nervous? You must be joking; he's not afraid of anything."

"Just goes to prove you never really know everything about anyone," Stuart said, looking pensive.

"I guess it all depends on what life throws at you," Will said. "We all change with life's experiences."

"That's too philosophical for me," Tim replied with a smile.

At last, with the last of the embers died down, and Will's parents already gone home, they reluctantly made ready for bed. It had been an enjoyable day. Tomorrow the work would begin.

The whole family threw themselves into the project with great enthusiasm. While Tim and Stuart started to lay the slates, one on each side of the farmhouse, Jason and Will filled the hods and kept the slaters supplied with slates.

Mrs Larkin, Penny, and Alice, along with Lizzy, Bill, and Eliza, were busy at the cottage. They were painting, filling, and rubbing down the walls, while the two men cut, pasted, and hung the wallpaper. By the end of the week, the inside of the cottage was totally renovated.

Over at the farmhouse, the roof was nearing completion, but time was up, and those from Sussex had to go back to harvest the last of the vegetables before the winter set in.

"I don't know how to thank you," Tim said as he saw them off on the train.

"Well, we might call on you to give us a hand next season," Jason replied. "We've put in a lot of soft fruits. They should crop well in the summer."

"You can rely on me," Tim replied.

Back at the house, it seemed strange and quiet without the Sussex contingent. Michael, who had the job of plastering some of the cottage and whitewashing the outside, said, "I can help you finish the farmhouse this weekend. But next week, I am on a job at Windsor, so I won't be at home."

"Well, there isn't much left to do to the farmhouse," Tim said. "I would think we could finish it in a weekend. Then I just have to get the cottage roof done. It seems like everything else has been done."

"Yes, Tim, and it looks a treat. The two grandads were dab hands at hanging the wallpaper, and there was a whole team of painters on the go." Michael had obviously enjoyed himself. "You should have seen Mrs Larkin; she had nearly as much paint on her as on the cupboards she was painting."

"Oh, heck. Full of runs, is it?" Tim inquired.

"I'm not saying. See for yourself."

Michael winked at his dad. Will smiled; he knew Michael was having his brother on. He had been over with Penny last evening to fix the curtain poles and saw what a good job had been done

"It looks like the weather is breaking up this week," Will said. "Definitely feels like rain. If you don't mind getting wet, I suggest we get the coal and hay deliveries done, then if it's dry, I'll give you a hand with the cottage next week."

"I would certainly appreciate that. It'll be difficult carrying the slates up as well as laying them." Tim brightened up. "You're a good egg, Dad."

"Not so good as you think: I'll lay the roof; you can carry the hods."

"I knew there was a snag somewhere," Tim said, laughing.

CHAPTER 24

The Return of the Two Larkin Brothers

℘ ℰ ℘

Mrs Larkin had bought the local papers and was busy going through the, situations vacant column.

"I do think we should start looking for work as soon as possible," she told Alice.

"Oh, Mum, don't panic. Tim hasn't done the roof yet."

"No," she replied, "but if we move in now, we'll be able to put buckets under the leaks."

"He didn't want our decorations to get spoiled; that's why he asked us not to decorate until the roof was done."

"I know, Alice, but how could we pass up on all that help that was available that week? "

"That's true; wasn't it wonderful the way they dropped everything to help us? But you mustn't worry too much; Will put one of those tarpaulins they use for the hay over the roof. It won't do to rush him. Anyway, his dad is going to give him a hand, probably next week if it's dry. There are some buckets in the roof space too. We must hope for the best."

Her mother sighed and said, "I suppose you're right. But I just want to get on with it."

"Well, pass me one of the papers, please. I'll see what I can find."

"You have a look. I can't see anything. But I don't really know what to look for. I know I don't want to end up charring."

"Do you fancy a factory? There is a job here for a machinist in the umbrella factory."

"I didn't see that one; shall we try?"

"Why not?" Alice replied, standing up and buttoning her coat. "It will be a start in the job hunt. I'll go ring for an appointment. The jobs may all be gone if we wait for the post."

"I'll come to the call box with you," her mother said. "We should tell them about our home dressmaking."

They set off together, feeling quite excited. The young lady who answered the phone said, "Please hold the line while I connect you to the manager."

"Good morning, can I help you?" a deep voice asked.

"We're calling about the job making umbrellas," Mrs Larkin said.

"Would you be able to come for an interview at 3:30 this afternoon? Ask for James Bostock."

Mrs Larkin said they would be there and then hung up. She could not believe her ears. "Just like that? They must be desperate for workers."

"Well, it could be that they advertised last week too, and today is the day for the interviews." Alice knew her mother had only had office cleaning jobs in recent years. But she also knew that no one could trim a hat or turn a hem as quickly as she could. Alice wasn't worried that her mother wouldn't suit the position but that she may fall short of what was expected.

In any event, her mother was hired as a machinist and finisher, and Alice was given the job of fitting the umbrella covers to the wire frames. They had to do some sample work. James Bostock seemed well-pleased, and for their part, they liked the surroundings Although it was an old building, it was clean and warm. The other ladies seem pleasant and the beautiful, coloured fabrics a joy to behold.

"We also manufacture parasols," Mr Bostock explained. "Most of them are exported to the colonies, of course."

True to his promise, Will helped Tim with the cottage roof. The weather also held for them, and by the following Saturday, it was complete. Alice and her mother were due to start their jobs on Monday. Sunday saw them busily loading their belongings onto one of the flat-bottomed coal carts; Tim had spread the tarpaulin he had used to protect the cottage roof across the floor of the cart, in case coal dust was lurking in the corners. With Penny and Will's help, the beds were in and the curtains up before it got dark. Alice had put the clothes they were to wear for work in a separate box. Food and tea things were installed in the kitchen and larder.

"We'll leave you to it now," Penny said, making for the door. "I expect you'll want an early night. Big day tomorrow."

"Thank you very much," Alice said. "It was kind of you to help us move."

"Good night, then, and good luck. Come on, Penny; the car is outside."

Will was ready to be off. It had been a long day.

"You, coming, Tim?" he asked.

"Do you mind if I go now, Alice?"

"No, I shall have an early night too."

Tim gave her a quick kiss and asked, "It all went okay, didn't it?"

"Marvellous," she replied. "See you tomorrow night, then."

Alice waved them off and went back indoors. Her mother was sitting in the armchair, looking very worried.

"What's the matter, Mum?"

"I am worried about tomorrow," she replied. "What if I can't do the job quickly enough?"

Alice enjoyed the company of the girls she worked with; she soon got into the swing of fitting the covers to the frames. Mrs Larkin proved to have a very artistic streak and was soon making covers for the fancy parasols; for the first time in her life, she was earning a decent wage. Each week, she worked a little more on preparing a room for George and Dick, who were expected very shortly. Tim had asked around for vacancies working in the open air. An estate he delivered to was looking to hire a trainee gamekeeper and an assistant gardener.

"It's good of you to take the trouble to find them positions," Mrs Larkin said, clearly pleased with him.

"It may not be what either of them want," he replied. "We'll have to see what they have to say about it."

Tim was having misgivings. He didn't know these brothers of Alice. Jim had been his friend, but he had never met his brothers.

"Dad said I can borrow the car to meet the ferry at Dover. It will be a bit of a squash, but if we put your mum in the front, you could squeeze in with Dick and George in the back. You'll want to meet them off the ferry, won't you?"

Alice gave him a hug and said, "Tim, you are a treasure," planting a kiss on his cheek.

"How long will the journey take, do you think?"

"Well, say the journey takes three hours. Better allow stopping time to cool the engine and have a cup of tea and something to eat, so five hours should be about right. What ferry are they catching, do you know?"

"Well, it says here, 'Arriving Dover 3 p.m.,'" Alice said; she now read fluently.

"Do you think we should take a picnic? We could have a good breakfast before we set off."

"That's a good idea, Alice. We ought to take food and drink in case we need to cool the engine miles from a café."

"I'll pack the picnic and flasks," Mrs Larkin said. "It will give me something to do. Take my mind off it for a while." She certainly looked flustered.

"Poor old Mum. You're just like a hen, gathering up her chicks." Alice was laughing at her mother.

"Don't tease, Alice; your mum has had a lot of worry with her boys."

"But that's just the point, Tim. They aren't boys anymore. They are men, and men don't like a lot of fuss."

"Don't they? You can make a fuss over me if you like."

"Now then, you two. No hanky-panky." Mrs Larkin stood in the kitchen doorway, waving the bread knife.

"Isn't she a dragon?" Tim exclaimed. "You really need brothers to protect you as well as your mother."

"Enough of your cheek, young Tim," and with that, Mrs Larkin disappeared into the kitchen, where she could be heard humming as she cut sandwiches.

The weather was fine and sunny as they journeyed through the Kentish countryside. Although the leaves had not started to colour, there was a feel of autumn in the air. The last of the flowers had that fluorescence that flowers have when the sun is not quite as hot.

When they finally stopped for their picnic, they chose a sunny bank out of the wind. Bumblebees were busy in the lady's slipper flowers. Sounds of cows lowing and cocks crowing came from the nearby dairy.

"I could stay here all day; it's a lovely spot."

Tim stretched and got up.

"Better press on, though; there may be a lot of traffic at the ferry quay."

Reluctantly, they reloaded the car and set off for Dover once more. The traffic was light, it being a weekday, with not too many people travelling to the coast. Conditions suited the car; apart from one fill-up, the radiator did not overheat, and they made good time.

After parking the car, they made their way to where passengers disembarked.

"What if we don't recognise them and we miss them all together?" Alice's mum was panicking again.

"We won't miss them. Alice wrote and told them we'd be here to meet them. They are going to meet us outside the waiting room." Tim smiled reassuringly at Mrs Larkin. "It's going to be alright. You don't need to worry."

"You're a good lad, Tim," she replied. "I don't know how we would have managed without you."

As the ferry docked, they could see two figures waving frantically.

"Is it them? I do hope they haven't missed the boat."

"It *is* them," Alice shouted excitedly.

In what seemed no time at all, there were two fresh-faced young men with that lovely glow that comes from being in the pure air of the Alps.

"Mum, Alice," they cried, enveloping them in big bear hugs and kisses. Their mother had tears of joy running down her face. Tim, standing to one side, was surprised by the love and affection this family had for one another (his family was much less demonstrative; he knew they loved him, but he had always been very reserved). He felt a twinge of envy and determined to be more demonstrative himself.

"This is Tim," Alice introduced him to her brothers. "Tim, this is George."

"Pleased to meet you, I'm sure."

"And this is Dick."

"We heard all about you from Jim," George said. "He said you waited until he was out of the country and then pinched our sister." George's eyes were twinkling as he said this.

"We haven't missed the wedding, have we?" Dick quipped.

"We haven't tied the knot yet," Tim replied.

"Well, I should look sharp if I were you before you lose her to someone else."

"In the spring," Tim replied. "We will get married in the spring."

Alice could hardly believe her ears.

"When did you decide that?" she asked.

"Just now; I can't take the risk I might lose you."

"Oh, I just love it when you're impetuous," she replied, planting a big kiss on his cheek. "I accept. Spring it is."

"Well, Jim will be home by then. I want him to be best man."

Now that he made his decision, Tim was rather pleased with himself. Last week, he had seen his dream of owning a piece of land come true. He had not told Alice yet. He wanted to divide it into yards to let out to the light industry. All the services were connected, and he was looking forward to collecting his rents. They should, he figured, cover the housekeeping expenses: another problem solved.

He felt a bit like celebrating, so he suggested, "How about fish and chips all round, on me?"

"Thanks, but I could murder a plate of fish and chips with mushy peas, bread and butter, and a cup of tea. Could you stretch to that?" George asked. "Dick and I are skint until we can get a job. I don't like to ask, but I'll see you alright when I can."

"You're not to worry about money," Mrs Larkin butted in. "I've saved some for you. It's not a lot, but it should see you through until you start work. Tim has found an estate that may take you both on; one to garden and one to be a gamekeeper."

"Well, if you want it, they are interested in you. I don't want to presume you'd take that kind of work." Tim felt uncomfortable. He didn't,want to offend these two young man. "Your mother asked me to look out for you," he said lamely.

But he need not have worried, for George immediately replied, "That's,really good of you, Tim. We have been out of circulation so, long, it will be difficult to get a place. I for one shall definitely,try for it. What about you, Dick?"

"It sounds great to me," Dick replied. "We both want to be out in the open air."

Tim was pleased his good intentions were not taken amiss, as he feared they might be. These brothers were very amiable chaps. He was sure he was going to like them.

They found a fish and chip shop and were soon tucking into large plates of freshly fried fish and chips, mushy peas, a mountain of bread and butter, and gallons of tea.

"That was great! First food since breakfast," Dick said, wiping his lips.

"What time was that?" Alice asked.

"About 4:30 this morning. We were on the train at 5:15."

"No wonder you were famished. What a long journey it must be." Alice, who had never been farther than a day trip to Southend until today, could not imagine a journey taking so long.

Travelling home, everyone was quiet. Looking in his mirror, Tim could see both brothers were asleep. Alice caught his eye and smiled. *I love you,* he mouthed silently.

Where upon Mrs Larkin, who he had thought was asleep, said, "Keep your eyes on the road, young man."

At that, Alice laughed, the boys woke up, and everyone wanted to know what the joke was.

It was almost dark when they finally arrived at the cottage. Mrs Larkin went inside and put the kettle on the gas; Tim lit the gas mantel, and Alice put a match to the fire.

It wasn't long before they were in front of the fire, enjoying a nice hot cup of tea. George and Dick had lots to tell them about Switzerland and the hostel they had stayed in while recuperating and skiing in the mountains.

"I thought you were there for your health, not a holiday," Alice quipped.

"Yes, but as we got better, we had to have more of the clear air. It was lovely in the mountains: streams, goats, cows with bells, and wonderful spring flowers, some even pushing their heads up through the snow. You would love it, Mum."

"I'm sure I would. But you'll be surprised when you see our garden."

"This seems a very comfortable home after the old place; how did you find it?" George asked.

"Ah, that is a long story. But be careful what you say. The landlord is sitting beside you."

"What, Tim? Is it yours?"

"Well, yes, I suppose it is. But it's your mum's home as long as she wants it."

"But where will you live when you wed?" George asked.

"I haven't had time to decide on it yet. I've only just announced the wedding."

Dick winked at Alice and said, "We'll soon have him sorted out for you."

Alice looked amused and said, "Don't tease him too much."

Tim soon made his excuses and left for home. He was tired yet felt elated. Now he had his land. Soon that would bring in an income. He had yet to tell his father what he been up to. Hopefully, Jim would be back in the spring. There was room for him in the cottage with his mother. Now that he had finished, he must start again, this time for a home for himself and Alice.

Tired as he was, he just could not get to sleep with everything going through his mind. At last, he got up and went downstairs to the kitchen. To his surprise, Will was sitting at the kitchen table, working out figures. He looked up as Tim entered.

"Hello, son; I am just trying to see if I can work out a weekly income for you. Your mum said Alice is worried she'd have to ask for every shilling. I agree that would be awful. But I thought of offering you a partnership, where we would divide the profits between us at the end of the year. What do you think?"

"Well, for a start, neither of us could wait a year for income. So how about if we agree on a weekly wage for us both? Then, at the end of the year, after expenses and renewals, we can have a bonus from the profits."

"Sounds good to me."

Will's voice reflected his relief. He relied on Tim's help and had been afraid he might lose him.

"By the way, I have started a business myself, but it won't make any difference to our working relationship."

"Go on; tell me about it."

"Well, I bought land along the Great West Road. I intend to split it into yards for light industry. I just wanted to do something on my own, prove I can help myself and stand on my own two feet." Then smiling at his dad, he delivered his punchline: "I didn't want to always be in the shadow of my old man's success."

Laughing, Will countered, "I'm really proud of you, Tim. You're a true brave."

Tim laughed. "Not that old Red Indian tale again. Is it really true?"

"Yes, but it seems a lifetime ago."

"You're a remarkable man, Dad. You've done a lot for me, and I think you're a true brave yourself."

They sat in companionable silence, drinking their tea. Then, they wended their way back to bed. Soon the only sound in the house was the ticking of the old grandfather clock and the steady breathing of the sleeping inhabitants.

CHAPTER 25

A Surprise for Penny

⌐ ℰ ⌐

Tim had a load of coal to deliver over to Southlands, a large house on the green at West Drayton. It was a cold, windy wet day. He was huddled up with his cap pulled down, his coat collar pulled up as high as he could get it. If the horse hadn't suddenly shied, he might never have seen the notice board in the hedge. He stopped the horse and got down to read it. His excitement rose as he read:

For Sale by Auction

Elizabethan house with Georgian facade.
Servants' quarters, stable and yard, walled garden,
hop houses, orchard, and paddock.
Freehold in one lot.

It was just what his dad was looking for. But somehow, he could not see his parents living in a big house like this.

That evening, he waited until his mother was busy in the kitchen.

"Dad, can I have a word with you?" he began. "Do you still want a mansion?"

"I certainly do. Your mother will never give me any peace until I get a large place. She wants to have the family to stay more often. It's such a bother, moving all the rooms around to fit everyone in. Family seems to get bigger every year."

"Well, I have found just the place."

"Go on. Where?" Will sounded very, excited.

"Closer than you think. Avenue House, on the green, is up for sale by auction."

"Don't say a word to your mother."

"Are you going to surprise her?"

"I don't know yet. But I'm determined to go to the auction. I know that house, but I never thought the family would part with it."

"Well, they have flown the nest. It is a big place to keep up."

"But think of the space. It could be virtually self-sufficient in fruit and veg. Even run as a smallholding."

Will was already turning over in his mind what he would do with the land. "On the other hand, we could have tennis parties and dances in the barn; in fact, lots of fun."

"Now then, Tim, calm down; don't get carried away. Life isn't all fun, you know."

"Come on, Dad, lighten up. Have fun and enjoy it."

Will drove over to view the house. Driving around the green, he realised what a splendid approach it had; the nearest house was Southlands, tucked away behind a row of trees.

But Avenue House faced out onto the green, the front covered in Virginia creeper, glowing red in the autumn sunshine. To one side was a shrubbery with a long white herbaceous border, skirting the path to the front door. The front was a rather plain Georgian, with long sash windows with internal shutters, some of which were closed, giving the house a forlorn look.

Will skirted the house, coming soon to a row of outbuildings, stables, and the walled garden. The walled garden was set out with espalier pears, peaches, apples, and apricots. The walls had been built to enclose hot pipes which ran directly from the boiler within the hot houses; here, an ancient vine pushed its way valiantly through the broken panes and nettles that now grew within the house. It would take some work to restore the garden and hot houses to their former glory. The cloches, although overgrown, were still whole. Rows of raspberries and gooseberry bushes were still visible, and overgrown strawberry plants spilled their runners over the soil.

Through the gate in the wall was a small field and beyond that a gate leading to two enormous trees: a walnut and a mulberry, which may have been there when James the First tried to introduce silkworms. Tennis courts were sheltered by the trees, and beneath the walnut tree was a seat which circled its girth.

Will sat and felt the quietness; this was, he decided, to be his refuge from daily cares. Plonk! He was suddenly roused from his daydreaming by a nut landing on the seat beside him. Reluctantly, he got up and made his way back through a gate into the yard, where there was yet more stabling and a barn for hay.

On this side of the house, which was the Elizabethan part, a black and white cottage was attached. Through the ancient timbers and small leaded windows, he could just make out armour and old muskets on the walls. It all had the feeling of not being lived in, as if he were stepping back in time.

He had not viewed inside, but his mind was made up. He had to have it, even if it meant spending all their savings. A little voice was prickling his conscience. What if Penny didn't like it? But Will silenced his fears. He meant to have this house, come what may.

During the following two weeks, Will became very on edge. He did his best to consolidate his assets, for he knew that if he succeeded with his bid at the auction, he must immediately find 10 percent of the purchase price and then pay the balance in one week. Penny was perplexed. Will's moods were up and down like Tower Bridge.

"What is the matter with your father?" she asked her sons.

Sworn to keep the secret, they shrugged their shoulders and suggested he was having a midlife crisis.

The day of the auction came. Will made some excuses to Penny about going to a meeting to discuss a hay contract. She still had not twigged what he was up to. But whatever it was, it was making him jittery.

The auction was to be held on the premises in the barn. Will took a seat in the back to assess the opposition. There were a good many people in the room, but they were mainly local people come to see what it would sell for, mostly just out of curiosity. The furnishings were to be auctioned later so the purchaser of the property could bid for the contents.

The auctioneer read out the terms of the auction. Out of the corner of his eye, Will saw Bob Smith making his way towards him and swore under his breath; trust him to have such a blabbermouth around at this moment. Distracted, he missed the opening bid. Two or three bids followed. Bob started to babble in his ear, so Will couldn't hear the auctioneer. In a desperate bid to join in, he raised his hand.

He heard the auctioneer saying, "Going, going gone. Name, please."

He was pointing at Will. He heard his voice answering in a croaky voice, "Long, Will Long."

He felt all eyes on him, some curious, as if to say, "How did you get all that money?" Others looked hostile, as if they resented him.

The usher came across and said, "Would you mind going along to the office, please?"

Will got up, excused himself, and pushed past the other people in his row. Groups of people were getting together in earnest conversation, breaking off to stare at him as he went past; he saw a sign, "Office this way," and followed it into a stable, which had been turned into a temporary office. The auctioneer got up from his desk and shook Will's hand.

"Please be seated, Mr Long. My clerk will be with you in a moment to sort out the details."

It seemed an age to Will before the clerk arrived, carrying some folders and the deeds. Will may have a looked confident on the outside, but his stomach was churning. How much had he spent? Would he have enough cash? And if not, where could he raise the balance in a week?

The auctioneer was talking.

"You did amazingly well for yourself. I quite expected the property to fetch far more."

"What did you think it would make, then?" Will asked, trying to get some idea of the purchase price.

"I couldn't possibly tell you that," he replied. "But I can say you got yourself a bargain."

Will relaxed a little bit. It could not be too bad if he had a bargain, could it?

"If you'd just sign the contract and confirm that is the correct figure that you bid for the property."

The clerk laid the papers before Will.

His eyes went straight to the final figure on the contract. In his head, he added on the commission to the bill of sale, and then a broad grin spread across his face.

The clerk smiled and said, "Well, I hope your missus is as pleased with your purchase as you are."

"She will love it, I am sure," Will replied.

"If you want help to get the garden sorted out, I could help at the weekend. I have an interest in the old place; my dad was the gardener for forty years."

"Then you must be Joe Price's lad. He was a friend of my dad."

"That's right; my name is Herbert."

"It's been a pleasure to meet you. You'll have the memory of how the garden was then. I would be very grateful if you would advise me on the restoration."

"I have Dad's effects, including the original garden plan."

Will was delighted. "That's fantastic, Herbert," he exclaimed.

The auctioneer was amused. "Did you buy it for the garden?" he asked.

"No, but the wife has had this thing about having a large house so our family can come and stay more often."

The auctioneer smiled and said, "That's not something I'd encourage my wife to do." He gathered his papers and said, "Good day, gentlemen."

"Now don't forget, Herbert," Will called. "After we move in, come and see me with those plans."

"I look forward to the project," he replied. "It would be great to see the garden as it was."

After he left, Will decided that he too had better be on his way.

Back home that night, Will was feeling pretty smug. He had his house and still had two thousand pounds to go towards the contents sale, to buy whatever Penny wanted. He fancied the armour and muskets himself. Some of the antiques and carpets and curtains were very desirable. But first, he had to get Tim and Michael to help him prepare the surprise for Penny. Will decided to take Penny for a ride in the trap to see the autumn colours. He would ride around the green, and as they approached the gates,

Tim and Michael would step forward and open them. Alice would be at the front door and invite Penny to view the house.

Then Will was going to step forward and give her the key, saying, "I'm glad you like the house because it's ours now."

Sunday came and the wind blew; clouds skittered across the sky, threatening to rain.

"Are you sure you want to go for a ride in the trap in this weather?" Penny was mystified; it was usually a job to get Will out for a ride, even in the sunshine.

"Don't keep on, woman," he replied. "Get your coat on; we're going out."

She seemed miffed at this and rode with him in silence.

Bother, he thought. *Now I have offended her.*

But as planned, when they approached the gates, their two smiling sons stepped out and opened them. Will drove the trap into the yard and stopped with a flourish.

"What are the family doing here?" Penny asked.

But before Will could answer, Alice came towards them.

She helped Penny down, saying as she did, "Do come and look at this lovely house."

"But whose house is it?" Penny asked.

Tim, Michael, and Alice all looked at Will. What could they say?

"Will, what's going on?"

"It's the mansion you wanted."

For a moment, Penny stood there, absolutely speechless. Then she started to laugh.

"Stop teasing," she said. "People would think we are Lord and Lady Muck."

"We are," Will replied, and everyone laughed.

They went inside and walked from room to room. Alice and Penny were so excited, studying the fabrics, hangings, and oriental carpets.

"What a fantastic treasure trove, Alice; just look at this." Penny had stopped by a table that displayed Millefiori paperweights under glass.

"I am sure they are French." Alice laughed. "It's no good asking me. The only expertise I have is with parasols."

"Parasols?" exclaimed Michael. "They are lovely fried in butter."

"Just listen to him," said Penny. "Not an ounce of decorum in him. If you want to be a gentleman, you must do better than that."

"A gentleman? To think you'll make him into one of them?" Tim was laughing.

"Stop taking the mickey out of Michael and help Penny to decide what she wants," Will said severely. But there was no mistaking the twinkle in his eye.

"Couldn't we buy the contents as they stand?" Penny wanted more time to decide what should be kept and what sold.

"I could ask the auctioneer." Will paused and then added, watching her face anxiously, "Thing is, I have spent most of the money."

"How much should we offer?" Penny asked. "I have some savings myself."

"How have you managed that?" Will exclaimed.

"My antiques have sold very well through the exchange and the mart."

"It will take more than pin money, though. At least a couple of thousand."

"I can manage that," Penny replied.

Alice, Tim, and Michael could hardly believe their ears.

"You made all that out of a few pieces of china and a few old pictures? You're a bloody marvel, woman."

Penny sighed. "I have been telling you that for years. But you just don't listen."

Alice, Tim, and Michael giggled, which turned into outright laughter when Will remarked, "What would I do without her? She's got me out of no end of scrapes."

"Well, that's settled then. Will, you must try to get a price for the lot. Even if we don't want it all, it will be a big boost to my stock." Penny was now moving on. "I haven't seen the bedrooms or the kitchen yet."

She was soon to find out. The grime of ages covered everything; crumbling plaster flaked off into the sinks; copper pans still hung on the walls, green with verdigris; mice droppings littered the floor; and the range was red with rust. Hanging on the wall was the original bell board.

"I'll be able to ring for my supper now," Will quipped.

"You'll wait for a long time, then. It will be bread and pull it, from now on. I shall be in the garden soaking up the sun."

"Not for a while, you won't." Tim opened, up, the shutters to reveal the sodden, overgrown shrubbery. It was raining cats and dogs. Nothing could dampen Penny's spirits. Everyone has dreams, but not many realise them as fully as Penny did this day.

"I have always dreamed of a home like this," she said, "where everyone could come and stay. A true family home. What a wonderful surprise." She gave Will a big hug.

"Steady on, Mum. It's a good job Alice's mother isn't here. She would soon put a stop to your behaviour, with her, 'No hanky-panky now.'" Tim was laughing.

"Give over, Tim; she is allowed a bit of excitement. After all, it isn't every day a maid becomes mistress of a grand house, is it?"

Alice sounded as excited as Penny, who was still staring into the overgrown shrubbery in a dreamy way.

"It's perfect, just perfect," she murmured.

.

Lightning Source UK Ltd.
Milton Keynes UK
UKHW011834061220
374547UK00009B/249